Old Quilts New Life

Old Quilts New Life

18 step-by-step projects inspired by
quilts from the American Folk Art Musuem

Sarah Fielke

CICO BOOKS
LONDON NEW YORK

This one's for Damo. Thank you darling.

Published in 2015 by CICO Books
An imprint of Ryland Peters & Small Ltd
20–21 Jockey's Fields, London WC1R 4BW
341 E 116th St, New York, NY 10029

www.rylandpeters.com

10 9 8 7 6 5 4 3 2 1

A CIP catalog record for this book is available from
the Library of Congress and the British Library.

ISBN: 978 1 78249 239 9

Printed in China

Editors: Erica Spinks and Alison Wormleighton

Designer: Alison Fenton
Photographer: Sue Stubbs
Illustrator: Stephen Dew

Art director: Sally Powell
Head of production: Patricia Harrington
Publishing manager: Penny Craig
Publisher: Cindy Richards

contents

introduction

This book has been a long time in the making. In fact, I think it's probably been brewing ever since I became infatuated with old quilts and their history, over 20 years ago. It may sound trite, but the idea of generations of women stitching their slow way through time makes me feel part of something so wide, ancient, and special. Of course, I don't mean just women who stitch quilts—I mean all stitchers everywhere—but quilters have a special place in my heart.

I have always loved history of all kinds, and I particularly love antique quilts—I love the patterns, the fabrics, the colors, and the stories behind them. I own a vast library of books about quilting, stitching, and textile design, most of which I have read from cover to cover. I have always drawn inspiration from old quilts and all of my books talk about that in one way or another. Here in *Old Quilts New Life* was the chance to connect antique quilts with my quilts, and also to help today's quilters connect with what has gone before and see the wealth of inspiration and knowledge there is to be gained from the study of quilts from the past.

I wrote this book using American quilts because they have a firm and tangible place in most people's minds. The quilts I have chosen to reinterpret in this book are all from the collection of the American Folk Art Museum in New York, and the pictures of the original quilts shown here are reproduced with their kind permission.

Each chapter shows one of the originals, with two quilts of my own making. My first quilt of the pair is my direct interpretation of the original quilt, but not an exact reproduction. All the patterns for these quilts and any changes I have made to the original designs are my own. For the second quilt in each pair, I have taken a design element from the original quilt and reinterpreted it as a modern quilt. Sometimes these links are very clear and sometimes I have taken just one element of the original to make a new and fresh design.

I hope you enjoy this book. I loved writing it, and I loved making the quilts for it, probably more so than any other book I have written. I like to think the makers of the original quilts might have approved, too.

Center Star Quilt
Artist unidentified
New England
1815–1825
Glazed wool
100½ x 98"
Collection American Folk Art Museum, New York
Gift of Cyril Irwin Nelson in honor of Robert Bishop, director (1977–1991),
American Folk Art Museum, 1986.13.1

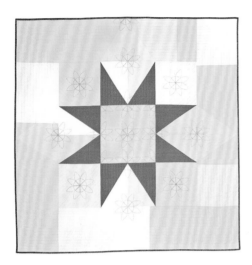

Almost Amish
Sarah's direct interpretation

Whole-cloth quilts are those made from large pieces of solid or printed cotton or wool. They typically have only small amounts of piecing, and the design and embellishment come from the quilting itself rather than the patchwork. Whole-cloth quilts were often made from plain cotton or from glazed wool; if printed cottons were used, the pieces were usually stitched carefully together to match the patterns, giving the appearance of a single piece of fabric rather than patches.

Contrary to popular belief, whole-cloth quilts were not usually made from only one piece of fabric. As with most quilting fabrics today, fabrics available at the time were

whole-cloth quilts

A Stitch in Time
Sarah's modern reinterpretation

not large enough to cover a whole bed with one width of fabric. This was because of the width of the looms that existed during the period. Therefore, the quilts were pieced either along the center or into three panels or, as with this example, as a very simple patchwork.

Most whole-cloth quilts are heavily quilted, traditionally using small quilting stitches. However, some are worked in trapunto, using cording and stuffing to make the space inside the quilting motifs stand away from the background.

This particular quilt was made in New England sometime between 1815 and 1825 by an unknown quilter. The quilting is worked over the central star in grids, medallions, and an intricate feathered border. If you look closely you can see all the places in the border where the quilter has pieced the fabrics together, and even one section where a different-colored patch has been joined.

While both of my quilts are very close in pieced design to the antique quilt, I have veered away from the traditional hand-quilting to utilize big stitch hand-quilting for Almost Amish, while A Stitch in Time has been heavily machine-quilted in both the positive and negative spaces for a modern twist.

almost amish

Antique? Oh no, this quilt is oh-so-modern with its solids and its negative space. And yet, Almost Amish is an exact copy of the original Center Star Quilt—the same star with the same balance of border. The style of the quilting helps to fast forward this beauty to the 21st century and places it squarely in the realm of Modern Quilting, while still keeping its roots exposed for all to see.

When I pieced this quilt and A Stitch in Time (see page 14), I used a lot of the same background fabrics for both tops. I had only a certain amount of each and I didn't want to buy more because I felt that making do with what I had was the perfect way to honor the mismatched background pieces of the original quilt. So Almost Amish has no red in the center of the star—I only had enough for the points!

Hand quilting very densely can be difficult and frustrating if you are just beginning. Take into account what fabrics you use to piece your quilt if you are going to hand-quilt. Almost Amish is all made from Oakshott solids, which are very soft and fine, and the backing is voile, also fine and easy to needle. The combination of the two made the quilting pleasurable and easy to work. I have used 100% cotton wadding with no scrim for all my hand-quilted quilts.

finished size

Double-bed size quilt or throw, 80½ in. (204.8 cm) square

Note All strips are cut across the width of the fabric from fold to selvage, and seams are stitched with right sides together using a ¼ in. (6 mm) seam allowance unless otherwise stated.
Note To make a queen-bed size quilt, add an 8 in. (20.3 cm) border all around in the same fabric as the star.

material requirements

- 24 in. (60 cm) red chambray fabric for star points
- 1¼ yd (1.2 m) each of five different cream and white fabrics for background
- 28 in. (72 cm) royal blue fabric for the binding
- 4⅞ yd (4.4 m) backing fabric
- 86 in. (219 cm) square cotton batting (wadding)
- Cotton thread for piecing
- One sheet of template plastic (see page 137 for templates)
- Pencil for tracing on template plastic
- Scissors for cutting template plastic
- Masking tape for marking quilting lines
- Crewel embroidery needles no. 9 for hand-quilting
- Aurifil Mako' Ne 12 weight cotton in light pink, hot pink, dark purple, and aqua for quilting
- Rotary cutter, mat, and ruler
- Sewing machine
- General sewing supplies

cutting

From the template plastic, cut:
- One Template A (circle)
- One Template B (flower petal)

From the red chambray fabric, cut:
- Four 11 x 16½ in. (28 x 42 cm) rectangles for star points. Cross-cut these rectangles diagonally once into eight triangles.

From the assorted cream and white fabrics, cut:
- One 20½ in. (52 cm) square for star center
- Four 15½ in. (39.4 cm) squares for star corners
- Four 11 x 16½ in. (28 x 42 cm) rectangles for star points. Cross-cut these rectangles diagonally once into eight triangles.
- Seven 15½ in. (39.4 cm) strips for borders

From the royal blue fabric, cut:
- Nine 3 in. (7.6 cm) strips for the binding

Tip You can mix the shapes you cut from different cream and white fabrics, and it is fine to cut a rectangle from one end of a border strip and then use the rest of the strip in the border.

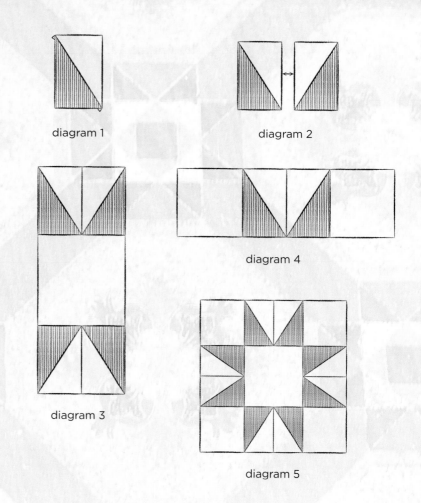

diagram 1

diagram 2

diagram 3

diagram 4

diagram 5

making the quilt

sewing and assembly

1. Sew the red and white/cream triangles together in pairs along the diagonal edges. Be aware that you need to allow for the seam allowance at the points of the triangles so, if necessary, mark the ¼ in. (6 mm) seam allowance on the triangles to help you match the points. The "ears" of the triangles will not match (see Diagram 1). Press the seams toward the red fabric. The piece should measure 10½ x 15½ in. (26.6 x 39.4 cm). Make eight rectangles.

2. Arranging the pieces on your design wall or work surface (see Tip on page 126), arrange two rectangles that face in opposite directions, with the red triangles angling outward (see Diagram 2). Sew the rectangles together along the center long edges to make star points. Press the seam to one side. Repeat for the other rectangles to make four star points.

3. Sew one set of star points to one side of the center square, and a second to the opposite side (see Diagram 3). Press the seams toward the star points.

4. Sew a 15½ in. (39.4 cm) white/cream corner square onto each end of the remaining two star points (see Diagram 4). Press the seams toward the red fabric.

5. Sew these star-point strips to the remaining sides of the piece assembled in step 3 (see Diagram 5). Press the seams toward the star points.

borders

6. Sew all the 15½ in. (39.4 cm) white/cream border strips (and partial strips if you have them) end-to-end to make one long strip, mixing the fabrics as you go. Cut a 15 in. (38.2 cm) length from the beginning of the strip and sew it to the other end. This will make the borders staggered instead of having all the same lengths of one fabric.

7. Trim two 50½ in. (128.3 cm) lengths from this strip. Fold the strips in half and mark the centers with pins. Mark two opposite sides of the quilt top in the same way. Matching the pins and the ends, with right sides together, pin the border strips to these two sides of the quilt top. Sew the borders in place and then press the seams toward the border.

8. From the remaining pieced border strip, cut two 80½ in. (204.5 cm) lengths. In the same way, pin and then sew the border strips to the remaining two sides of the quilt.

backing, quilting, and binding

9. Cut the backing fabric crosswise in half into two 86 in. (219 cm) pieces. Remove the selvages and sew the pieces together along the long edges to make the backing. Press the seam open and press the backing.

10. Layer the backing, batting (wadding), and quilt top, following the instructions on page 131.

11. Starting in the center of the quilt, use Templates A and B to mark the quilting lines with a chalk pencil (see Diagram 7). Using Aurifil Mako' Ne 12 weight cotton in dark purple, hot pink, and aqua, quilt the shapes following the instructions on pages 131–132. Using masking tape as a guide to quilt along, quilt straight lines, 1 in. (2.5 cm) apart, in light pink and hot pink cotton (see Diagram 6).

12. Bind the quilt, following the instructions on page 133.

diagram 6

a stitch in time

The professional quilting on this quilt was done in a very modern fashion, by using the stitches to fill in each area. The intricate patterns are used to great effect and in different combinations to decorate the sections of the star and the background, creating texture and interest.

Modern machine-quilting, to my mind, is being defined in two very separate categories. The quilters who machine-quilt their own tops on domestic sewing machines at home are a fast-growing group. These quilters are becoming more and more skilled, and incredible work is being done. Modern machine-quilters using professional longarm machines are forging new territory by creating their own designs and inspiring home machine-quilters to try more complex patterns with their domestic machines.

finished size

Small single-bed size quilt or wall hanging, 50½ in. (128.4 cm) wide x 80½ in. (204.8 cm) long

Note All strips are cut across the width of the fabric from fold to selvage, and seams are stitched with right sides together using a ¼ in. (6 mm) seam allowance unless otherwise stated.

material requirements

- 1¼ yd (1.2 m) charcoal fabric for center square and star points
- 1¼ yd (1.2 m) each of three different cream and white fabrics for background
- 22 in. (56 cm) red-and-white striped fabric for the binding
- 4⅞ yd (4.4 m) backing fabric
- 56 x 86 in. (143 x 219 cm) piece cotton batting (wadding)
- Cotton thread for piecing
- Rotary cutter, mat, and ruler
- Sewing machine
- General sewing supplies

cutting

From the charcoal fabric, cut:
- Four 11 x 16½ in. (28 x 42 cm) rectangles for star points. Cross-cut these rectangles diagonally once into eight triangles.
- One 20½ in. (52 cm) square for star center

From the assorted cream and white fabrics, cut a total of:
- Four 15½ in. (39.4 cm) squares for star corners
- Four 11 x 16½ in. (28 x 42 cm) rectangles for star points. Cross-cut these rectangles diagonally once into eight triangles.
- Three 15½ in. (39.4 cm) strips for borders

From the red-and-white striped fabric, cut:
- Seven 3 in. (7.6 cm) strips for the binding

making the quilt
sewing and assembly

1. Sew the charcoal and white/cream triangles together in pairs along the diagonal edges. Be aware that you need to allow for the seam allowance at the points of the triangles so, if needed, mark the 1/4 in. (6 mm) seam allowance on the triangles to help you match the points. The "ears" of the triangles will not match (see Diagram 1, page 12). Press the seams toward the charcoal fabric and then trim the rectangles to measure 10½ x 15½ in. (26.6 x 39.4 cm) (see Diagram 2, page 12). Make eight rectangles.

2. Arranging the pieces on your design wall or work surface (see Tip on page 126), arrange two rectangles that face in opposite directions, with the charcoal triangles angling outward (see Diagram 3, page 12). Sew the rectangles together along the center long edges to make star points. Press the seam to one side. Repeat for the other rectangles to make four star points.

3. Sew one set of star points to one side of the center square, and a second to the opposite side (see Diagram 4, page 12). Press the seams toward the star points.

4. Sew a 15½ in. (39.4 cm) white/cream corner square onto each end of the remaining two star points (see Diagram 5, page 12). Press the seams toward the charcoal fabric.

5. Sew these star-point strips to the remaining sides of the piece assembled in step 3 (see Diagram 6, page 12). Press the seams toward the star points.

borders

6. Sew all the 15½ in. (39.4 cm) white/cream border strips (and partial strips if you have them) end-to-end to make one long strip, mixing the fabrics as you go. Cut a 15 in. (38.2 cm) length from the beginning of the strip and sew it to the other end. This will make the borders staggered instead of having all the same lengths of one fabric.

7. Trim two 50½ in. (128.3 cm) lengths from this strip. Fold the strips in half and mark the centers with pins. Mark the top and bottom of the quilt top in the same way. Matching the pins and with right sides together, pin the border strips to the top and bottom of the quilt top. Sew the borders in place and then press the seams toward the border.

backing, quilting, and binding

8. Cut the backing fabric crosswise in half into two 86 in. (219 cm) pieces. Remove the selvages and sew the pieces together along the long edges to make the backing. Press the seam open and press the backing.

9. Layer the backing, batting (wadding), and quilt top, following the instructions on page 131. If you are going to have the quilt professionally machine-quilted, do not layer it.

10. Quilt as desired. Mine was professionally custom machine-quilted with intricate swirls, grids, flowers, and geometric patterns in different combinations to fill each area of the quilt.

11. Bind the quilt, following the instructions on page 133.

Sunburst Quilt
Probably Rebecca Scattergood Savery (1770–1855)
Philadelphia
1835–1845
Cotton
125½ x 118½"
Collection American Folk Art Museum, New York
Gift of Marie D. and Charles A.T. O'Neill, 1979.26.2
Photo by Terry McGinnis

Flash
Sarah's direct interpretation

Although I have made many star quilts, and many quilts using diamonds, I had never made a Sunburst quilt. I love star quilts probably more than any other, and the Sunburst Quilt on the opposite page was so stunning that I wasn't able to resist the temptation any longer.

The quilt was made between 1835 and 1845, probably by Rebecca Scattergood Savery, a member of a prominent Philadelphia Quaker family, well known for her quilting. It was made using the English paper piecing method, in which each piece of fabric is basted over a paper template and the pieces are then whipstitched together by hand. The method was common during this period, especially for quilts made using the same template shape, such as hexagons, pentagons, or diamonds, over and over. While it

a burst of sunshine

Spark
Sarah's modern reinterpretation

is time-consuming, the template provided for my Flash quilt (see page 136) could easily be used for the same method if you removed the seam allowance.

Of the six quilts attributed to Rebecca Scattergood Savery that are currently in quilt collections, three are of a Sunburst design. Given that this quilt contains about 2,900 diamonds, another one almost 4,000, and yet another, spectacular example has 6,708, the quilts say much about her dedication, and her condition in life. Quilts such as these take a lot of time and a lot of fabric, two things that would have been a luxury for a woman in the early 1800s. At just over 1,500 pieces, the pattern for Flash is a little more achievable, but no less beautiful and enjoyable to piece.

flash

Spots and stripes and things that fizz! That's what this quilt is made of. All my favorite things, in my favorite colors. You better believe this quilt is going on my bed!

I'll be honest—this quilt is not easy to piece. If you haven't sewn with diamonds before, I highly recommend marking the seam line on each piece carefully with a sharp pencil before you sew, even if you're machine-piecing. It's very easy to be just that little bit out, which with all those seams on all those angles adds up to a lot. Remember when you are pressing to do it carefully so you don't stretch all the bias edges.

finished size

Queen-size (UK: king-size) bed quilt, 91 in. (231 cm) square

Note All strips are cut across the width of the fabric from fold to selvage, and seams are stitched with right sides together using a ¼ in. (6 mm) seam allowance unless otherwise stated.

material requirements

- 8 in. (21 cm) red checked fabric for center and corners (Fabric 1 and 24)
- 6 in. (15 cm) red-on-white polka-dot fabric for Fabric 2
- 8 in. (21 cm) white-on-pink polka-dot fabric for Fabric 3
- 12 in. (30 cm) pink check fabric for Fabric 4
- 12 in. (30 cm) pink-on-white polka-dot fabric for Fabric 5
- 14 in. (35 cm) pink graphic print fabric for Fabric 6
- 18 in. (45 cm) white-on-mauve polka-dot fabric for Fabric 7
- 20 in. (51 cm) blue-and-white checked fabric for Fabric 8
- 22 in. (56 cm) blue-and-white striped fabric for Fabric 9
- 22 in. (56 cm) blue-and-white graphic print fabric for Fabric 10
- 26 in. (66 cm) aqua graphic print fabric for Fabric 11
- 28 in. (71 cm) white-on-aqua polka-dot fabric for Fabric 12
- 30 in. (76 cm) green-and-white graphic print fabric for Fabric 13
- 32 in. (82 cm) green-and-white striped fabric for Fabric 14
- 32 in. (82 cm) green-on-white polka-dot fabric for Fabric 15
- 36 in. (91 cm) white-on-green polka-dot fabric for Fabric 16
- 1⅛ yd (1 m) orange-and-white striped fabric for Fabric 17
- 20 in. (51 cm) white-on-orange polka-dot fabric for Fabric 18
- 18 in. (45 cm) white-on-yellow polka-dot fabric for Fabric 19
- 18 in. (45 cm) yellow-and-white checked fabric for Fabric 20
- 12 in. (30 cm) olive-on-white polka-dot fabric for Fabric 21
- 12 in. (30 cm) olive-and-white striped fabric for Fabric 22
- 8 in. (21 cm) olive-and-white checked fabric for Fabric 23
- 30 in. (76 cm) red-and-white striped fabric for the binding
- 8¼ yd (7.5 m) backing fabric
- 98 in. (2.5 m) square cotton batting (wadding)
- Cotton thread for piecing
- Rotary cutter, mat, and ruler
- Sewing machine
- General sewing supplies
- 45-degree diamond ruler (optional)
- One sheet of template plastic (optional—see page 136 for templates)
- Pencil for tracing on template plastic (optional)
- Scissors for cutting template plastic (optional)

cutting

From all the fabrics, you will cut 2⅝ in. (6.7 cm) strips and then cross-cut these into 45-degree diamonds. You can either use Template A for this or use the 45-degree line on your general patchwork ruler. There are various methods of cutting diamonds, but I find a 45-degree diamond ruler such as an Easy Eight the simplest, quickest, and most accurate method.

Tip If you are using a directional print such as a stripe, remember that you need reverse pairs of diamonds if you want the prints to meet at the edge of each panel. To achieve this, simply make sure that you cut the diamonds from a doubled strip (as the fabric came off the bolt); don't open the cut strip to a single fabric layer.

From the template plastic, cut:
• One Template A

From Fabric 1 and 24, cut:
• Three 2⅝ in. (6.7 cm) strips. Cross-cut these strips into twenty-four diamonds.

From Fabric 2, cut:
• Two 2⅝ in. (6.7 cm) strips. Cross-cut these strips into sixteen diamonds.

From Fabric 3, cut:
• Three 2⅝ in. (6.7 cm) strips. Cross-cut these strips into twenty-four diamonds.

From Fabric 4, cut:
• Four 2⅝ in. (6.7 cm) strips. Cross-cut these strips into thirty-two diamonds.

From Fabric 5, cut:
• Four 2⅝ in. (6.7 cm) strips. Cross-cut these strips into forty diamonds.

From Fabric 6, cut:
• Five 2⅝ in. (6.7 cm) strips. Cross-cut these strips into forty-eight diamonds.

From Fabric 7, cut:
• Six 2⅝ in. (6.7 cm) strips. Cross-cut these strips into fifty-six diamonds.

From Fabric 8, cut:
• Seven 2⅝ in. (6.7 cm) strips. Cross-cut these strips into sixty-four diamonds.

From Fabric 9, cut:
• Eight 2⅝ in. (6.7 cm) strips. Cross-cut these strips into seventy-two diamonds.

From Fabric 10, cut:
• Eight 2⅝ in. (6.7 cm) strips. Cross-cut these strips into eighty diamonds.

From Fabric 11, cut:
• Nine 2⅝ in. (6.7 cm) strips. Cross-cut these strips into eighty-eight diamonds.

From Fabric 12, cut:
• Ten 2⅝ in. (6.7 cm) strips. Cross-cut these strips into ninety-six diamonds.

From Fabric 13, cut:
• Eleven 2⅝ in. (6.7 cm) strips. Cross-cut these strips into 104 diamonds.

From Fabric 14, cut:
• Twelve 2⅝ in. (6.7 cm) strips. Cross-cut these strips into 112 diamonds.

From Fabric 15, cut:
• Twelve 2⅝ in. (6.7 cm) strips. Cross-cut these strips into 120 diamonds.

From Fabric 16, cut:
• Thirteen 2⅝ in. (6.7 cm) strips. Cross-cut these strips into 128 diamonds.

From Fabric 17, cut:
• Fourteen 2⅝ in. (6.7 cm) strips. Cross-cut these strips into 136 diamonds.

From Fabric 18, cut:
• Seven 2⅝ in. (6.7 cm) strips. Cross-cut these strips into sixty-four diamonds.

From Fabric 19, cut:
• Six 2⅝ in. (6.7 cm) strips. Cross-cut these strips into sixty diamonds.

From Fabric 20, cut:
• Six 2⅝ in. (6.7 cm) strips. Cross-cut these strips into fifty-two diamonds.

From Fabric 21, cut:
• Four 2⅝ in. (6.7 cm) strips. Cross-cut these strips into forty diamonds.

From Fabric 22, cut:
• Four 2⅝ in. (6.7 cm) strips. Cross-cut these strips into thirty-two diamonds.

From Fabric 23, cut:
• Three 2⅝ in. (6.7 cm) strips. Cross-cut these strips into twenty-four diamonds.

From the red-and-white fabric, cut:
• Nine 3 in. (7.6 cm) strips for the binding

making the quilt
sewing and assembly

Note Lay out each panel on your design wall or work surface (see Tip on page 126) before you begin sewing. Work on one panel at a time so that you can pick the pieces up, sew the row, and then put them back. As there are so many pieces in this quilt, it's very easy to get the pieces out of order but if you work in this way you should be able to stay organized. Drawing the ¼ in. (6 mm) seam line on all the diamonds before you begin will ensure you know precisely where you are stitching to and from.

1. There are two different types of panels in this quilt: center panels and corner panels. The four center panels are made first, and then the four corner panels. Referring to the quilt photograph, lay out a center panel from the center outward, beginning with one red checked diamond for Row 1 (see Diagram 1).

2. Sew the diamonds together into diagonal rows. Be sure to line up the ¼ in. (6 mm) points on the diamonds and cut off the "ears" after you sew each row, to ensure a smooth finish (see Diagram 2). Press the seams in each row to one side. Be careful not to stretch the bias edges.

3. Sew the rows together into a panel (see Diagram 3). The diamonds for row 17 will hang out longer than the quilt will be when finished; they will be trimmed later. Press the seams in the panel to one side. Take care not to stretch the bias edges—placing the panel somewhere flat after piecing will help prevent stretching. Make four panels in this way.

diagram 1

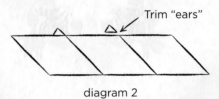

Trim "ears"

diagram 2

diagram 3

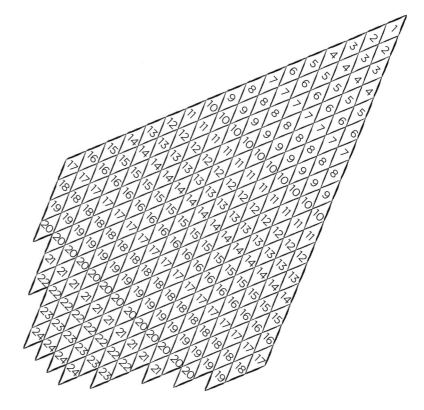

diagram 4

4. In the same way as for the center panels, make four corner panels (see Diagram 4 for diamond orientation and color order).

5. Sew a corner panel and a center panel together. Trim the ragged ends of the center panel and the bottom of the corner panel off straight (see Diagram 5), using the line formed by the diamond points in the center panels as a guide. Press the seam to one side.

Tip In step 5, I actually trimmed to ¾ in. (1.9 cm) outside the seam lines, rather than the normal ¼ in. (6 mm) outside the seam lines. Then, after the quilt was quilted, I used this extra fabric outside the seam lines to help me make the quilt square and enable me to cut to an accurate ¼ in. (6 mm) from the diamond points before binding. However, if you prefer, you can trim to ¼ in. (6 mm) in step 5.

6. In the same way, sew together the next pair of panels. Now sew the two joined pairs of panels together along the center seam and trim again. Press the seam to one side. Repeat with the other half of the quilt, and then sew the two halves together along the center seam. Press the seam to one side. Trim any remaining edges so that the quilt is square (see Diagram 6).

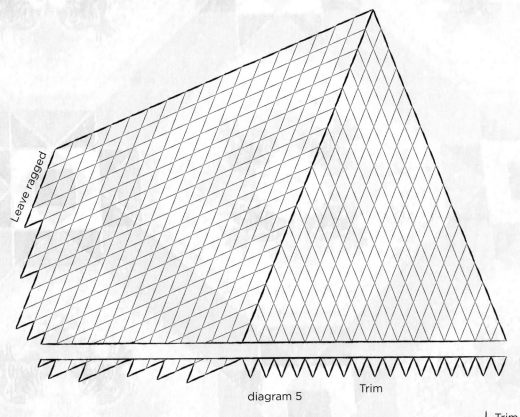

diagram 5

Leave ragged

Trim

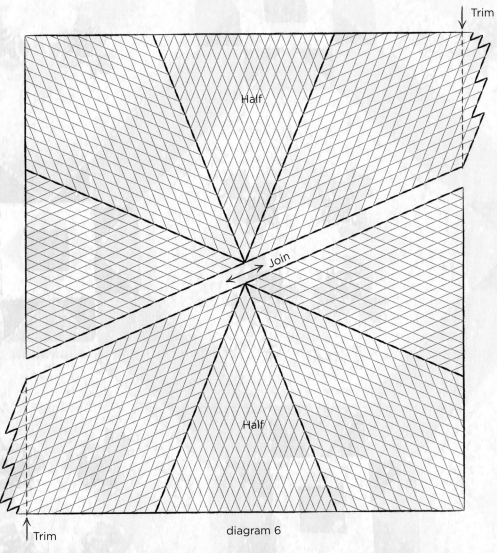

Trim

Half

Join

Half

Trim

diagram 6

backing, quilting, and binding

7. Cut the backing fabric crosswise into three 98 in. (250 cm) pieces. Remove the selvages and sew the pieces together along the long edges to make the backing. Press the seams open and press the backing.

8. Layer the backing, batting (wadding), and quilt top, following the instructions on page 131. If you are going to have the quilt professionally machine-quilted, do not layer it.

9. Quilt as desired. Mine was professionally machine-quilted in an all-over pattern of little leaves.

10. Bind the quilt, following the instructions on page 133.

spark

This quilt is like the spark of the idea for the Flash quilt. A little burst of color and light before the fireworks went off—that's how I saw it when I was designing it, anyway! I love the contrast of the natural linen that makes these lovely fabrics "float." If you want your quilt to be larger, adding an 8 in. (20.5 cm) border of alternating pieced floral and linen strips, which have been cut to the same size as the background strips, would give you a striking striped border for a queen-sized option.

finished size

Double-bed size quilt, 80½ in. (204.8 cm) square

Note All strips are cut across the width of the fabric from fold to selvage, and seams are stitched with right sides together using a ¼ in. (6 mm) seam allowance unless otherwise stated.

material requirements

- 4 in. (10 cm) purple fabric for Fabric 1
- 8 in. (20 cm) green floral fabric for Fabric 2
- 16 in. (40 cm) pink graphic fabric for Fabric 3
- 4 in. (10 cm) green striped fabric for Fabric 4
- 8 in. (20 cm) checked fabric for Fabric 5
- 4 in. (10 cm) pink floral fabric for Fabric 6
- 8 in. (20 cm) pink striped fabric for Fabric 7
- 2¼ yd (2.1 m) light blue-on-white polka-dot fabric for Fabric 8
- 4¼ yd (4 m) linen for background
- 28 in. (70 cm) purple-and-white striped fabric for the binding
- 4⅞ yd (4.4 m) backing fabric

- 86 in. (227 cm) square cotton batting (wadding)
- Cotton thread for piecing
- Rotary cutter, mat, and ruler
- Sewing machine
- General sewing supplies
- 45-degree diamond ruler (optional)
- One sheet of template plastic (optional—see page 136 for templates)
- Pencil for tracing on template plastic (optional)
- Scissors for cutting template plastic (optional)

cutting

From all the fabrics, you will cut 3⅜ in. (8.6 cm) strips and then cross-cut these into 45-degree diamonds. You can either use Template A for this or use the 45-degree line on your general patchwork ruler. There are various methods of cutting diamonds, but I find a 45-degree diamond ruler such as an Easy Eight the simplest, quickest, and most accurate method. If you are using a directional print, see the Tip on page 22 of Flash.

From the template plastic, cut:
• One Template A

From Fabric 1, cut:
• One 3⅜ in. (8.6 cm) strip. Cross-cut this strip into eight diamonds.

From Fabric 2, cut:
• Two 3⅜ in. (8.6 cm) strips. Cross-cut these strips into sixteen diamonds.

From Fabric 3, cut:
• Four 3⅜ in. (8.6 cm) strips. Cross-cut these strips into thirty-two diamonds.

From Fabric 4, cut:
• One 3⅜ in. (8.6 cm) strip. Cross-cut this strip into eight diamonds.

From Fabric 5 cut:
• Two 3⅜ in. (8.6 cm) strips. Cross-cut these strips into sixteen diamonds.

From Fabric 6, cut:
• One 3⅜ in. (8.6 cm) strip. Cross-cut this strip into eight diamonds.

From Fabric 7, cut:
• Two 3⅜ in. (8.6 cm) strips. Cross-cut these strips into sixteen diamonds.

From Fabric 8, cut:
• Twenty-three 3⅜ in. (8.6 cm) strips. Cross-cut these strips into 184 diamonds.

From the linen, cut:
• Forty three 3⅜ in. (8.6 cm) strips. Cross-cut these strips into the following lengths:
eight strips, each 22 in. (56 cm)
eight strips, each 20 in. (51 cm)
eight strips, each 19 in. (48 cm)
eight strips, each 18 in. (46 cm)
eight strips, each 17 in. (43 cm)
eight strips, each 16 in. (41 cm)
eight strips, each 15 in. (38 cm)
sixteen strips, each 13 in. (33 cm)
eight strips, each 11 in. (28 cm)
eight strips, each 10 in. (26 cm)
eight strips, each 9 in. (23 cm)
eight strips, each 8 in. (21 cm)
eight strips, each 5 in. (13 cm)

From the purple-and-white striped fabric, cut:
Nine 3 in. (7.6 cm) strips for the binding

making the quilt
sewing and assembly

Note Lay out each panel on your design wall or work surface (see Tip on page 126) before you begin sewing. Work on one panel at a time so that you can pick the pieces up, sew the row, and then put them back. As there are so many pieces in this quilt, it's very easy to get the pieces out of order but if you work in this way you should be able to stay organized. Drawing the ¼ in. (6 mm) seam line on all the diamonds before you begin will ensure you know precisely where you are stitching to and from.

1. There are two different types of panels in this quilt, the left and the right—by sewing a pair of panels and then sewing them together into a square, you can't get confused by the orientation of the diamonds.

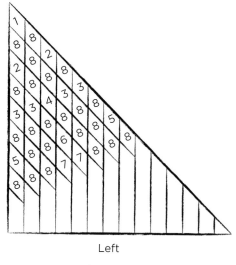

Left

diagram 1

Referring to the quilt photograph (see page 31), arrange the diamonds and linen strips for a left panel from the center outward, beginning with a Fabric 1 diamond at the center (see Diagram 1).

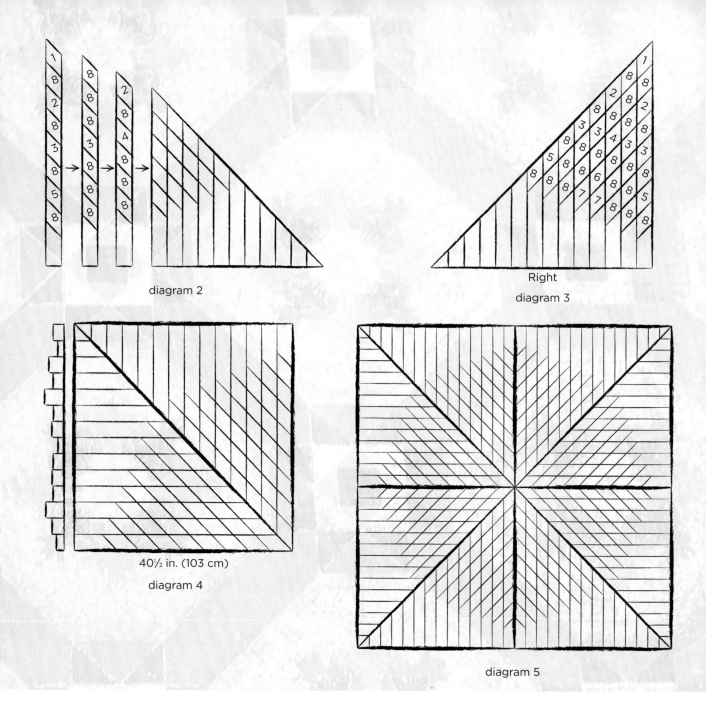

diagram 2

Right
diagram 3

40½ in. (103 cm)

diagram 4

diagram 5

2. Sew the diamonds together into rows (see Diagram 2). Be sure to line up the ¼ in. (6 mm) points on the diamonds and cut off the "ears" after you sew each row, to ensure a smooth finish. Trim the linen from behind the bottom diamond in each row. Press the seams in each row to one side. Be careful not to stretch the bias edges.

3. Sew the rows together into a panel, carefully matching the seams (see Diagram 2). The linen strips will hang out at odd lengths, which is fine as long as all the diamonds are meeting correctly; they will be trimmed later. Press the seams in the panel to one side, taking care not to stretch the bias edges. Make four panels in this way.

4. In the same way as for the left panels, make four right panels with the diamonds in the opposite direction (see Diagram 3).

5. Sew the left and right panels together along the diagonal seam in pairs (see Diagram 4). Trim the pairs to measure 40½ in. (103 cm) square, using the 45-degree diagonal seam as your guide for an accurate square.

6. Sew two square units together into a rectangle to make half the quilt. Press the seam to one side. Repeat with the other half of the quilt, and then sew the two halves together along the center seam, matching all the seams as you go (see Diagram 5). Press the seam to one side.

backing, quilting, and binding

7. Cut the backing fabric crosswise into two 86 in. (227 cm) pieces. Remove the selvages and sew the pieces together along the long edges to make the backing. Press the seam open and press the backing.

8. Layer the backing, batting (wadding), and quilt top, following the instructions on page 131. If you are going to have the quilt professionally machine-quilted, do not layer it.

9. Quilt as desired. Mine was professionally machine-quilted in an all-over swirling pattern.

10. Bind the quilt, following the instructions on page 133.

Whig Rose Quilt
Abigail Hill (dates unknown)
Probably Indiana
1857–1858
Cotton
79³⁄₄ x 70"
Collection American Folk Art Museum, New York
Gift of Irene Reichert in honor of her daughter, Susan Reichert Sink,
and granddaughter, Heather Sink, 1992.13.1
Photo by Matt Hoebermann

The Whig Rose pattern (also sometimes called Rose of Sharon) used in Abigail Hill's quilt (opposite) is thought by some to have originated from the Tudor Rose used by the kings of England. The Whig Rose, however, was associated with politics. The Whigs were an American political party formed in 1833 in opposition to President Andrew Jackson's Democratic party, and women of the era were sometimes known to declare their political leanings through the quilts they made.

Four-block appliqué quilts, like this one, were most popular between 1850 and 1900. A four-block quilt is created when the quilt-maker repeats a single motif, often quite complex, in four distinct blocks to make the main quilt area. Appliqué borders were sometimes, but

Sweet Home
Sarah's direct interpretation

political leanings

not always, added. Quilts in this style usually featured a floral design of roses, vines, or swags. Eagles and birds were also popular motifs.

Often four-block quilts were created in a red and green color scheme on a white background, sometimes with the addition of a bright pink or yellow highlight, as this quilt was. The color scheme was chosen for the stability of the colors. The madder-red fabrics used were dyed in Turkey; the red dye used was stable, and remained bright over many years. Chrome yellow and cheddar were used for the yellows, and the green was known as "poison green." At this time, the poison green would have been created by dyeing fabric yellow, and then overdyeing with blue dye. Over time the greens can fade to blue or beige, but this quilt has remained bright, and the colors are still true.

Sweet Home, my direct interpretation of the Whig Rose Quilt, was a delight for me to design. Drawing the shapes and planning the appliqué is where I'm in my element. I was delighted when I realized that using the graphic shapes in black and white to make use of the negative space for Positives and Negatives would keep the tradition while breaking the mold.

Positives and Negatives
Sarah's modern reinterpretation

sweet home

I loved the Whig Rose quilt as soon as I saw it. The blocks are just the kind of appliqué I love, and the birds are so lovely—I couldn't wait to start. If you enjoy appliqué, you will love this quilt, too, although I fully appreciate that it's a huge amount of work. To give your quilt the same scrappy appearance as mine, be sure to choose a wide range of different sized prints, from spots and checks to large florals and conversationals.

finished size

Queen-size (UK: king-size) bed quilt, 93½ in. (237.8 cm) square

Note All strips are cut across the width of the fabric from fold to selvage, and seams are stitched with right sides together using a ¼ in. (6 mm) seam allowance unless otherwise stated.

material requirements

- 2¼ yd (2.1 m) each of three white textured fabrics (I used voiles)
- 1 yd (1 m) each of two yellow-and-white fabrics for block borders
- Four fat quarters of different greens for stems in center blocks
- 24 in. (61 cm) green fabric for stems in the borders
- 10 in. (26 cm) each of four different red fabrics for Template A pieces
- 3½ yd (3.2 m) in total of a wide selection of different red fabrics for center flowers, small flowers, tulips, buds, and small birds
- Four 4½ in. (11.4 cm) squares of yellow fabric for the centers of center flowers
- 10 in. (26 cm) plain yellow for small flower centers
- A wide selection of different green scraps for leaves, buds, and tulips
- 8 in. (20.3 cm) each of four different greens for center-flower leaves
- Four 6 in. (15.2 cm) squares of different pink fabrics for date
- Four 10 in. (26 cm) squares of different pink fabrics for Template E pieces
- 20 in. (51 cm) red fabric for vases
- 10 in. (26 cm) pink fabric for vase centers
- 4 in. (10.2 cm) pink fabric for vase ripples
- Four 10 in. (26 cm) pieces of different green fabrics for birds
- Four 5 in. (12.7 cm) squares of different pink fabrics for birds' wings
- Scraps of pink, red, and yellow fabrics for birds' tails, berries, and birds' crests

- 1 yd (1 m) of green fabric for the binding
- 8¼ yd (7.5 m) backing fabric
- 100 in. (254 cm) square cotton batting (wadding)
- Eight sheets of template plastic (see pages 142–148 for templates)
- Pencil for tracing on template plastic
- Scissors for cutting template plastic
- Fabric scissors
- Hera marker for making bias strips
- Silver gel pen
- Appliqué glue
- Straw needles for appliqué
- Cotton thread to match appliqué fabrics
- Small, sharp scissors for trimming appliqué
- Cotton thread for piecing
- Masking tape for marking quilting lines
- Crewel embroidery needles no. 9 for hand quilting
- Aurifil Mako' Ne 12 weight cotton in white, pink, and green for quilting
- Small piece of thin cardboard (a cereal box is ideal)
- Aluminum foil
- Rotary cutter, mat, and ruler
- Sewing machine
- General sewing supplies

cutting

Note When cutting out the templates, be sure to mark them with the appropriate letter on the right side. If you have not tried my method of needle-turn appliqué, read page 127 carefully before cutting or sewing anything, following the instructions for tracing and cutting the appliqué fabrics. Even if you have done needle-turn appliqué before, read the project instructions carefully before starting.

From the template plastic, cut:
- One Template A (center flower)—This is a half-template, so trace it twice (once in reverse), with the dotted lines meeting, to make a full circle.
- One Template B (small flower)
- One Template C (leaf)
- One Template D (small flower center)
- One Template E (medium center flower)
- One Template F (center leaf)
- One Template G (center flower middle)
- One Template H (vase)
- One Template I (vase ripple)—This is a half-template, so trace it twice (once in reverse), with the dotted lines meeting.
- One Template J (vase center)
- One Template K (small bird)
- One Template L (left-hand bird)
- One Template M (left-hand bird wing)
- One Template N (right-hand bird)
- One Template O (right-hand bird wing)
- One Template P (right-hand bird crest)
- One Template Q (left-hand bird berry)
- One Template R (right-hand bird tail)
- One Template S (right-hand vase tulip)
- One Template T (right-hand vase tulip top)
- One Template U (top border bud)
- One Template V (top border bud leaf)
- One each of the numbers for date (templates are provided for 2015)

From two of the white textured fabrics, cut:
- Two 23½ in. (59.7 cm) squares from each fabric
- Two 16 in. (40.6 cm) strips from each fabric

From the other white textured fabric, cut:
- Five 16 in. (40.6 cm) strips

From the two yellow-and-white fabrics, cut:
- Eight 4½ in. (11.4 cm) strips from each fabric

From the four fat quarters of different green fabrics, cut:
- Eight ¾ in. (1.9 cm) bias strips from each fabric for the stems in the center blocks, following the instructions on page 129

From the 24 in. (61 cm) of green fabric, cut:
- ¾ in. (1.9 cm) bias strips for the stems in the borders, to measure approximately 17½ yd (16 m), following the instructions on page 129

From the green binding fabric, cut:
- Eleven 3 in. (7.6 cm) strips for the binding

Using Template A, cut:
- Four in different red fabrics for center blocks

Using Template B, cut:
- Thirty-two in different red fabrics for center blocks
- Twenty-six in different red fabrics for borders

Using Template C, cut:
- Sixty-four in different green fabrics for center blocks
- Ninety-seven in different greens for borders

Using Template D, cut:
- Thirty-two in plain yellow for center blocks
- Twenty-six in plain yellow for borders

Using Template E, cut:
- Four in different pink fabrics for center blocks

Using Template F, cut:
- Four from each of four different green fabrics (sixteen leaves in total) for center blocks

Using Template G, cut:
- Four from each of four different red fabrics (sixteen in total) for center blocks

Using Template H, cut:
- Two in red fabric for borders

Using Template I, cut:
- Two in pink fabric for borders

Using Template J, cut:
- Two in pink fabric for borders

Using Template K, cut:
- Twelve in different red fabrics for borders—six with right side up and six reversed

Using Template L, cut:
- Two in different green fabrics for the borders—one with right side of template facing up and one with template reversed

Using Template M, cut:
- Two in different pink fabrics for the borders—one with right side of template facing up and one with template reversed

Using Template N, cut:
- Two in different green fabrics for the borders—one with right side of template facing up and one with template reversed

Using Template O, cut:
- Two in different pink fabrics for the borders—one with right side of template facing up and one with template reversed

Using Template P, cut:
- Two in different pink fabrics for borders—one with right side up and one reversed

Using Template Q, cut:
- Two in different red fabrics for borders

Using Template R, cut:
- Two in different yellow fabrics for borders—one with right side up and one reversed

Using Template S, cut:
- Two in different green fabrics for borders

Using Template T, cut:
- Two in different red fabrics for borders

Using Template U, cut:
- Two in different red fabrics for borders

Using Template V, cut:
- Two in different green fabrics for borders

Using the number templates, cut:
- One of each in different pink fabrics

making the quilt

sewing, assembly, and appliqué of center blocks

1. Trim four strips from each of the yellow-and-white strips, each 23½ in. (59.7 cm) long. Fold two of the strips in half and mark the centers with pins. Mark two opposite sides of a 23½ in. (59.7 cm) white textured square in the same way. Matching the pins, the ends, and with right sides together, pin these border strips to the square, pinning along the length of the borders; this step is important to keep the borders flat. Sew the borders in place and then press the seams toward the border.

2. Trim the remaining eight yellow-and-white strips into 31½ in. (80.1 cm) lengths. Pin and then sew two of these to the other two sides of the square in the same way as in step 1. Press the seams toward the border.

3. Attach the remaining twelve strips to the other three white squares in the same way as in steps 1 and 2.

4. Using the Hera marker, make bias strips for the appliqué stems for the center blocks following the instructions on page 129. Trim the seam allowances to ⅛ in. (3 mm) before pressing.

5. Fold and then press a pieced square into quarters on the straight grain of the fabric. Refold and then press the square into quarters on the diagonal.

6. On your design wall or work surface (see Tip on page 126), place a Template A piece in the center of the block, using the pressed lines and the quilt photograph as guides. Arrange four Template F leaves so that the edges of each leaf are well under the edge of the flower, and the points of each leaf run along the pressed straight lines.

7. Press one of the bias strips for the stems into a left-facing curve following the instructions on page 129. Place the strip under the Template A piece, along the pressed diagonal line. Curve it between two Template F leaves and around to the left. Trim another bias strip to a shorter length and curve it to the right. Place the end of this strip under the left-curving stem about halfway up. These strips are too narrow to allow you to use the appliqué glue because it would be difficult to stitch through where the glue came to the edge of the stem, so thread-baste the stems in place (see page 131). Repeat with all thirty-two stems.

8. Prepare the Template D pieces into perfect circles using the foil technique on page 128. Appliqué the circles to the Template B flowers.

Tip Appliquéing the yellow circles on the small red flowers makes a good carry-around project. Open the pressed circles as you are ready to glue and then appliqué them. This ensures the creases won't disappear from the fabric as you carry them around and you have lovely, sharp edges. When completed, you can glue all the flowers to the blocks with the circles already sewn in place.

9. Place a Template B flower over the end of each bias stem. Place the Template C leaves along each stem as shown in the quilt photograph.

10. Make the center of the large flower for each center block using one of the 4½ in. (11.4 cm) yellow squares and four of the Template G pieces. Fold the square in quarters along the diagonals and then place it on a cutting mat. Put a pin through the two points of a Template G arc. Line up the points with the crease lines on the corner of the square. You should be able to stand up the pins in the cutting mat. Repeat with the other three Template G arcs, matching the points. Carefully remove the pins and glue the pieces in place on the square, appliquéing only the inside edges of the Template G pieces. Turn the square to the back and trim the yellow fabric from behind the red arcs. Appliqué this unit to the center of Template E. Make four in this way.

11. Place the Template E piece on top of the Template A piece. When everything is in place, carefully lift the edges of the appliqué and put small dots of glue on the appliqué fabrics without moving them out of place. To ensure you can still turn the seam allowance under, do not put the glue too close to the edges. Note that you should always start with the piece that is underneath.

12. When the glue has dried (after about two minutes), finger-press around the gel pen line of the first appliqué shape. Thread a straw needle with thread to match the appliqué fabric, and knot the end of the thread. Following the instructions on pages 127–128, appliqué around the edges of the piece. Appliqué the stems first, and then Template A. Turn the square over to the back and carefully cut the background fabric away from behind Template A, ¼ in. (6 mm) from the stitching line. Then appliqué Template E, cut away the excess fabric from behind, appliqué Template G, and then cut away again. Continue in this manner to appliqué all the pieces to the square. Press the appliqué. Complete four blocks in this way.

13. Arrange the blocks so that two different yellow borders alternate. Pin and then stitch the blocks into pairs, pressing the seams of each pair in opposite directions. Pin and then stitch the pairs together, matching the seams. Press the seam to one side.

sewing, assembly, and appliqué of borders

14. Make the twenty-six Template B flowers with appliquéd Template D circles, as in step 8.

15. Make approximately 17½ yd (16 m) of ¾ in.- (1.9 cm-) wide green bias strips for the stems, following the instructions on page 129.

side borders

16. Sew the 16 in. (40.6 cm) white textured border strips end-to-end to make one long strip, removing the selvages and alternating the three different fabrics. Trim into two 62½ in. (159 cm) lengths. Pin and then sew the strips to the left-hand and right-hand sides of the quilt top, in the same way as in step 1. Press the seams toward the border.

17. Mark the center of the left-hand border with a pin. Fold a Template H vase in half vertically and position it with the base of the vase on the outer edge of the quilt top and the center lines matching. Remove the pin and glue the vase in place.

18. Referring to the quilt photograph, place a Template J vase center and a Template I vase ripple on the Template H vase, and glue in place. Repeat these two steps on the right-hand side of the quilt. The vases are reference points for the remaining appliqué pieces.

19. Referring to the quilt photograph, place the Templates K–R birds pieces on the right-hand side and left-hand side of the quilt, looking away from the vases.

20. In the left-hand vase, place a piece of vine coming straight up out of the vase for about 8 in. (20.3 cm). Place a Template B flower over the top of the stem and tuck the other end under the vase. Baste the stem in place and glue the flower.

21. Repeat step 20 for the right-hand vase. On either side of this flower, add two Template S tulips and two Template T tulip tops, each with stems curving to the side. Baste the stems and glue the tulips in place.

22. Using the photo of the quilt as a guide, start placing the stem on the lower half of the left-hand side of the quilt. When you get to the end of the border, stop basting the stem about 3 in. (7.6 cm) from the end of the border and leave a long piece of stem hanging. Referring to the quilt photograph, add the flowers, leaves, and stems, and then glue (or baste, in the case of stems) the pieces in place. Do the same for the upper half of the left-hand border. Appliqué the pieces in place to 3 in. (7.6 cm) from the end of the border. Repeat with the right-hand side of the quilt, noting that the appliqué pieces are different.

top and bottom borders

23. After you have completed the side border appliqué, measure the quilt top across the quilt through the center. It should measure 93½ in. (237.8 cm). From the remaining border strip, cut two pieces to this measurement. Mark the centers, and pin and then sew the borders to the top and bottom of the quilt, ensuring the loose bias pieces are clear of the seams.

24. Fold the quilt top in half to find the center of the bottom border. Center the numbers "2015" to either side of the center mark, with each piece about 1 in. (2.5 cm) apart. Glue and then appliqué the numbers.

25. Referring to the photograph of the quilt for placement, arrange the loose pieces of vine around the corners of the borders and along to the numbers. Baste in place. Arrange the stems, flowers, and birds and then baste and glue them in place. Appliqué all the shapes on the bottom border.

26. Fold the quilt top in half to find the center of the top border. Place a Template U bud and Template V bud leaf facing away from the center line on either side, about 2 in. (5 cm) from the center line. Glue in place. Arrange the stems around the corners of the border and all the way to the buds, crossing them over at the top. Baste the stems in place. Place and then appliqué all the shapes on the top border. Press the quilt top and remove the basting stitches from all the stems.

backing, quilting, and binding

27. Cut the backing fabric crosswise into three 98 in. (249 cm) pieces. Remove the selvages and sew the pieces together along the long edges to make the backing. Press the seams open and press the backing.

28. Layer the backing, batting (wadding), and quilt top, following the instructions on page 131.

29. Using Aurifil Mako' Ne 12 weight pink cotton, outline-quilt around the appliqué shapes, following the instructions on pages 131–132. Using masking tape as a guide, quilt straight lines 1 in. (2.5 cm) apart in white thread across the surface of the whole quilt top.

30. Bind the quilt, following the instructions on page 133.

positives and negatives

To me, this quilt feels like an echo. So many times, while working on the quilts for this book, I have glanced at their antique inspirations and wondered what the maker was thinking, or for whom or why they made the quilt. It must be something about the white, black, and fading grays that make this quilt feel reflective and slightly melancholy. I have used a tone-on-tone white fabric for the appliqué to give it a little bit of depth. The backgrounds are solids in graduating shades of gray.

I would love to see this as a crib (cot) quilt with red appliqué on white, with the borders grading out to pink. It would be so pretty!

finished size

Wall hanging or crib (cot) quilt, 54 in. (137.4 cm) square

Note All strips are cut across the width of the fabric from fold to selvage, and seams are stitched with right sides together using a ¼ in. (6 mm) seam allowance unless otherwise stated.

material requirements

- 32 in. (82 cm) tone-on-tone white fabric for appliqué
- 32 in. (82 cm) plain black fabric for quilt center
- 20 in. (51 cm) light gray fabric for Border 1
- 24 in. (61 cm) medium gray fabric for Border 2
- 24 in. (61 cm) dark gray fabric for Border 3
- 20 in. (51 cm) multicolored fabric for binding
- 3½ yd (3.2 m) backing fabric
- 62 in. (158 cm) square cotton batting (wadding)
- Four sheets of template plastic (see pages 143–145 for templates, which are templates A, B, C, and F used for Sweet Home)
- Pencil for tracing on template plastic
- Scissors for cutting template plastic
- Fabric scissors
- Hera marker for making bias strips
- Masking tape for marking quilting lines
- Crewel embroidery needles no.9 for hand quilting
- Aurifil Mako Ne 12 weight cotton in white and light gray
- Silver gel pen
- Appliqué glue
- Straw needles for appliqué
- Cotton thread to match appliqué fabrics
- Small, sharp scissors for trimming appliqué
- Cotton thread for piecing
- Rotary cutter, mat, and ruler
- Sewing machine
- General sewing supplies

cutting

Note When cutting out the templates, be sure to mark them with the appropriate letter on the right side. If you have not tried my method of needle-turn appliqué, read page 127 carefully before cutting or sewing anything, following the instructions for tracing and cutting the appliqué fabrics. Even if you have done needle-turn appliqué before, read the project instructions carefully before starting.

From the template plastic, cut:
- One Template A (center flower)
- One Template B (small flower)
- One Template C (leaf)
- One Template F (center leaf)

From the white tone-on-tone fabric, cut:
- One Template A for center flower
- Eight Template B for small flowers
- Sixteen Template C for leaves
- Four Template F for center leaves
- Eight ¾ in. (1.9 cm) bias strips following the instructions on page 129

From the black fabric, cut:
- One 32 in. (82 cm) square

From the light gray fabric, cut:
- Four 4½ in. (11.4 cm) strips

From the medium gray fabric, cut:
- Five 4½ in. (11.4 cm) strips

From the dark gray fabric, cut:
- Five 4½ in. (11.4 cm) strips

From the multicolored fabric, cut:
- Six 3 in. (7.6 cm) strips for the binding

making the quilt

sewing

1. Make bias strips for the appliqué stems following the instructions on page 129. Trim the seam allowances to ⅛ in. (3 mm) before pressing.

appliqué

2. Fold and then press the black square into quarters on the straight grain of the fabric. Refold and then press the square into quarters on the diagonals.

3. On your design wall or work surface (see Tip on page 126), place the center flower in the center of the black square, using the pressed lines and the quilt photograph as guides. Arrange the four center leaves so that the edges of each leaf are well under the edge of the flower, and the points of each leaf run along the pressed straight lines.

4. Press one of the bias strips into a left-facing curve following the instructions on page 129. Place the strip under the center flower, along the pressed diagonal line. Curve it up between two center leaves and

around to the left. Trim another bias strip to a shorter length and curve it to the right. Place the end of this strip under the left-curving stem about halfway up. These strips are too narrow to allow you to use the appliqué glue because it would be difficult to stitch through where the glue came to the edge of the stem, so thread-baste the stems in place instead (see page 131). Repeat with all the stems.

5. Place a small flower over the end of each bias stem. Place the leaves along each stem as shown in the quilt photograph. Check that the appliqué is at least 2½ in. (6.3 cm) in from the edges of the black fabric, to allow for trimming later.

6. When everything is in place, carefully lift the edges of the appliqué and put small dots of glue on the appliqué fabrics without moving them out of place. To ensure you can still turn the seam allowance under, do not put the glue too close to the edges.

7. When the glue has dried (after about two minutes), finger-press around the gel pen line of the first appliqué shape. Thread a straw needle with thread to match the appliqué fabric, and knot the end of the thread. Following the instructions on pages 127–128, appliqué around the edges of each piece until you have sewn all the pieces to the black square. Remove the basting stitches from the stems.

8. When the appliqué is complete, turn the quilt top over to the back and carefully cut the background fabric away from behind the flowers and leaves, ¼ in. (6 mm) from the stitching line.

9. Press your appliqué and trim the square to 30 in. (76.2 cm).

borders

Border 1

10. Trim two of the light gray strips into 30 in. (76.2 cm) lengths. Fold the strips in half and mark the centers with pins. Mark two opposite sides of the quilt top in the same way. Matching the pins, the ends, and with right sides together, pin the border strips to the quilt top, pinning along the length of the borders; this step is important to keep the borders flat. Sew the borders in place and then press the seams toward the border.

11. Trim the remaining two light gray strips into 38 in. (96.6 cm) lengths. Pin and then sew these to the other two sides of the quilt top in the same way as in step 10. Press the seams toward the border.

Border 2

12. Trim two of the medium gray strips into 38 in. (96.6 cm) lengths. Pin, sew, and then press the borders to opposite sides of the quilt top, as in step 10.

13. Sew the remaining medium gray strips end-to-end to make one long strip. Trim into two 46 in. (117 cm) lengths. Pin, sew, and then press the borders to opposite sides of the quilt top, as in step 11.

Border 3

14. Sew all the dark gray strips end-to-end to make one long strip. Trim into two 46 in. (117 cm) lengths. Pin, sew, and then press the borders to opposite sides of the quilt top, as in step 10.

15. Trim the remaining strips into two 54 in. (137.4 cm) lengths. Pin, sew, and then press the borders to opposite sides of the quilt top, as in step 11.

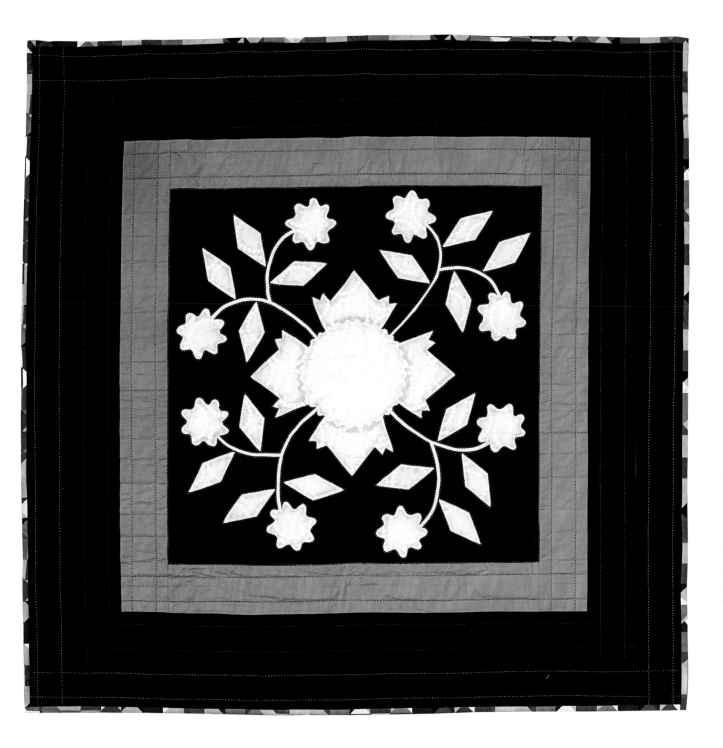

backing, quilting, and binding

16. Cut the backing fabric crosswise into two 62 in. (158 cm) pieces. Remove the selvages and sew the pieces together along the long edges to make the backing. Press the seam open and press the backing.

17. Layer the backing, batting (wadding), and quilt top, following the instructions on page 131. If you are going to have the quilt professionally machine-quilted, do not layer it.

18. Using Aurifil Mako Ne 12 weight white cotton, outline quilt around the applique shapes, following the instructions on page 131. Using masking tape as a guide, quilt straight lines 1 in. (2.5 cm) inside the seams along all the borders using light gray thread.

19. Bind the quilt, following the instructions on page 133.

Sunflowers and Hearts Quilt
Artist unidentified
Possibly New England
1860–1880
Cotton
85 x 91"
Collection American Folk Art Museum, New York
Gift of Frances and Paul Martinson, 1994.2.1
Photo by Matt Hoebermann

I've Got Sunshine
Sarah's direct interpretation

Appliqué is my favorite kind of stitching. I love the quiet repetition, the long hours spent creating pictures from fabric, and the lovely, tactile finished piece. It's hardly surprising that the old quilts that most often catch my eye are the appliqué designs.

The Sunflowers and Hearts quilt, opposite, has been on my "to do" list for a long time. It's the kind of quilt that makes me want to drop everything and start cutting templates. Actually choosing which appliqué quilts to remake and reinterpret for this book was by far the hardest task for me—I would gladly have made them all!

sunflowers and hearts

Smile, Darn Ya
Sarah's modern reinterpretation

The antique quilt was made during the appliqué revival of the mid- to late 1800s mentioned in the previous chapter. It features the reds and greens so fashionable at the time. The small addition of the cheery yellow color makes this quilt sing.

This quilt is a lovely example of the use of folk art symbols. Sunflowers can symbolize warmth and happiness, loyalty and longevity, while the hearts obviously represent love. While this is nothing but my flight of fancy, given these symbols I'd like to think that this quilt was made for the wedding of a young couple. Whatever the reason for the stitching, I'm sure the maker enjoyed the creation of this cheery quilt as much as I have enjoyed designing and stitching its counterparts.

i've got sunshine

On a cloudy day, this cheery quilt could easily brighten your mood. The antique quilt is such a delight that the temptation was just to make mine the same! But that would be cheating, so instead I have chosen a soft pink field for my sunflowers.

I purposely used different pinks for the background. Many antique quilts are made from what the user had at hand, and I have tried to be careful not to run to the quilt shop every time I need an extra few meters of fabric. These pinks were all in my stash and they sit so nicely together.

This quilt would look vibrant with text fabrics for the backgrounds and very bright sunflowers. It would also be truly lovely in soft reproduction fabrics on a gray or a natural linen background. Whatever you choose, the sunflowers are sure to shine!

finished size

Queen-size (UK: king-size) bed quilt, 92½ in. (235 cm) square

Note All strips are cut across the width of the fabric from fold to selvage, and seams are stitched with right sides together using a ¼ in. (6 mm) seam allowance unless otherwise stated.

material requirements

- 1½ yd (1.4 m) each of three different pink fabrics for backgrounds and outer border
- 1⅞ yd (1.8 m) extra pink fabric for background, setting triangles, and outer border
- 1½ yd (1.4 m) multicolored striped fabric for sashing
- 6 in. (15 cm) blue polka-dot fabric for cornerstones
- 1¼ yd (1.2 m) green polka-dot fabric for sunflower leaves and stems
- One 8 in. (20.4 cm) square each of fifteen assorted yellow fabrics for large sunflowers, or 26 in. (66 cm) single yellow fabric
- One 6 in. (15.2 cm) square each of twenty assorted yellow fabrics for small sunflowers, or 20 in. (50 cm) single yellow fabric
- One 6 in. (15.2 cm) square each of fifteen assorted pink patterned fabrics for large sunflower centers, or 20 in. (51 cm) single pink fabric
- One 4 in. (10.2 cm) square each of twenty assorted pink patterned fabrics for small sunflower centers, or 10 in. (25.5 cm) single pink fabric
- 124 1½ x 3½ in. (3.8 x 8.9 cm) assorted green fabric pieces for leaves
- One 5 in. (12.7 cm) square each of thirty-nine assorted hot pink fabrics for outer hearts, or 26 in. (66 cm) single hot pink fabric
- One 3 in. (7.6 cm) square each of thirty-nine assorted blue fabrics for hearts, or 10 in. (25.5 cm) single blue fabric
- 30 in. (77 cm) green fabric for bias stems
- 1 yd (1 m) pink-and-blue striped fabric for binding
- 8¼ yd (7.5 m) backing fabric (see Tip)
- 98 in. (2.5 m) square piece cotton batting (wadding)
- Three sheets of template plastic (see page 134–136 for templates)

- Pencil for tracing on template plastic
- Scissors for cutting template plastic
- Cardstock
- Fabric scissors
- Hera marker for making bias strips
- Roll of aluminum foil
- Silver gel pen
- Appliqué glue
- Straw needles for appliqué
- Cotton thread to match appliqué fabrics
- Cotton thread for piecing
- Masking tape for marking quilting lines
- Crewel embroidery needles no. 9 for hand quilting
- Aurifil Mako' Ne 12 weight cotton in dark pink, blue, and light pink for quilting
- Rotary cutter, mat, and ruler
- Sewing machine
- General sewing supplies

Tip For the backing I have specified three 98 in. (2.5 m) lengths, which is 8¼ yd (7.5 m), but it would be only 16 in. (40.5 cm) short across the width if you used just two drops of fabric. Therefore, if preferred, rather than buying three lengths, you could just use two lengths—5½ yd (5 m)—and then piece some other fabrics up the center of the backing.

cutting

Note If you have not tried my method of needle-turn appliqué, read page 127 carefully before cutting or sewing anything. Even if you have done needle-turn appliqué before, read the project instructions carefully before starting.

From the template plastic, cut:
• One Template A (leaf and stem)
• One Template B (large sunflower)
• One Template C (small sunflower)
• One Template D (large sunflower center)
• One Template E (small sunflower center)
• One Template F (small leaf)
• One Template G (outer heart)
• One Template H (inner heart)
Mark the templates with the appropriate letter on the right side.

From the three pink background fabrics, cut:
• Two 15½ in. (39.4 cm) strips from each fabric. Cross-cut these six strips into twelve 15½ in. (39.4 cm) squares.
• Cut the remainder of these fabrics into 10 in. (25.5 cm) strips for the outer border.

From the extra pink fabric, cut:
• One 15½ in. (39.4 cm) square
• Two 26 in. (66 cm) squares
• Two 13¼ in. (33.7 cm) squares
• Cut the remainder of this fabric into 10 in. (25.5 cm) strips for the outer border.

From the multicolored striped fabric, cut:
• Twenty-six 2 in. (5.1 cm) strips. Cross-cut eighteen of these strips into thirty-six 2 x 15 in. (5.1 x 38.2 cm) pieces. Set the other strips aside.

From the blue polka-dot fabric, cut:
• Two 2 in. (5.1 cm) strips. Cross-cut these strips into twenty-eight squares.

From the green polka-dot fabric, cut:
• Thirteen Template A for leaves and stems, cutting ¼ in. (6 mm) outside template

From the assorted yellow fabrics, cut:
• Fifteen Template B for large sunflowers, cutting ¼ in. (6 mm) outside template
• Twenty Template C for small sunflowers, cutting ¼ in. (6 mm) outside template

From the assorted pink patterned fabrics, cut:
• Fifteen Template D large sunflower centers, cutting ¼ in. (6 mm) outside template
• Twenty Template E small sunflower centers, cutting ¼ in. (6 mm) outside template

From the assorted green scrap fabrics, cut:
• 124 Template F small leaves, cutting ¼ in. (6 mm) outside template

From the assorted hot pink fabrics, cut:
• Thirty-nine Template G outer hearts, cutting ¼ in. (6 mm) outside the template. Do not cut the center out of the heart.

From the assorted blue fabrics, cut:
• Thirty-nine Template H inner hearts, cutting ¼ in. (6 mm) outside template

From the green fabric, cut:
• Seventeen 1 in. (2.5 cm) bias strips following the instructions on page 000. Cross-cut these bias strips into eight 22 in. (56 cm) strips and sixteen 9 in. (23 cm) strips.

From the pink-and-blue striped fabric, cut:
• Eleven 3 in. (7.6 cm) strips for the binding

making the quilt
appliqué

Sunflower blocks

1. Using the foil technique (see page 128), prepare the large and small sunflower centers to make them perfect circles.

2. Measure 2 in. (5.1 cm) from the bottom left-hand corner of a 15½ in. (39.4 cm) pink background square. Place the bottom of the leaf and stem there. Arrange the leaf and stem, large sunflowers, and large sunflower centers in a pleasing layout, ensuring the top of the stem is completely underneath the sunflower.

3. Carefully lift the edges of the appliqué and put small dots of glue on the appliqué fabrics without moving them out of place. To ensure you can still turn the seam allowance under, avoid putting the glue too close to the edges.

4. Place three hot pink outer hearts in the corners of the block, with the point of the heart ¾ in. (1.9 cm) from the corner, and the center of the heart running along the diagonal of the block. Glue the hearts in place without cutting the centers out of the hearts. Do not glue the blue hearts on yet.

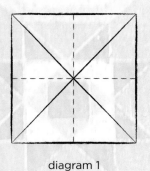

diagram 1

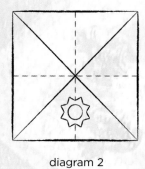

diagram 2

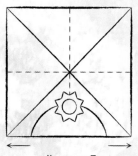

diagram 3

diagram 4

5. When the glue has dried (about two minutes) finger-press around the gel pen line of the first appliqué shape. Thread a straw needle with thread to match the appliqué fabric, and knot the end of the thread.

6. Following the instructions on pages 127–128, appliqué around the outside of the stem and leaf shape. In the same way, appliqué the large sunflower to the background fabric.

7. When the appliqué is complete, turn the quilt top over to the back and carefully cut the background fabric away from behind the large sunflower, ¼ in. (6 mm) from the stitching line, to reduce bulk.

8. Appliqué the large sunflower center in place. Turn over to the back and cut the excess fabric away from behind the sunflower center, as in step 7.

9. Appliqué the outside of each hot pink outer heart in place. Cut away the inside of each heart ¼ in. (6 mm) inside the outline, so that the background fabric shows in the center. You may have to pull the glue away to do this. Appliqué the center of each heart in place.

10. Glue the blue inner hearts inside the hot pink outer hearts, and appliqué in place.

11. Make thirteen large sunflower blocks as shown in steps 2–10. Trim the blocks to 15 in. (38.2 cm) square.

setting triangles

12. With an iron, press one of the pink 26 in. (66 cm) squares into quarters along the diagonals. Open out the square and finger-press it into quarters along the straight of grain in both directions (see Diagram 1).

13. Center a small sunflower on the finger-pressed line that runs through the middle of one of the resulting quarter-square triangles (see Diagram 2).

14. Make sixteen 9 in. (23 cm) and eight 22 in. (56 cm) curved bias strips for stems, following the instructions on page 129. Set the eight long ones aside for the outer border.

15. Position a 9 in. (23 cm) curved bias stem so one end is 5 in. (12.7 cm) from the outer corner of the triangle, and the other under the side of the small sunflower; position a second one on the other side of the small sunflower in the same way (see Diagram 3). Position four leaves on each stem, with the ends under the stems. Glue and then appliqué the pieces in place.

16. In the same way as for the large sunflowers (step 7), cut away the background fabric from the small sunflower.

17. Appliqué the small sunflower center in place. Turn to the back and cut the excess fabric away behind the sunflower center.

18. Repeat steps 13 and 15–17 for the other three setting triangles on this square, and then repeat steps 12, 13, and 15–17 for the other pink 26 in. (66 cm) square. Cut both squares into quarter-square triangles along the ironed creases (see Diagram 4), yielding eight triangles.

Corner triangles
19. With an iron, press one of the pink 13¼ in. (33.7 cm) squares in half along one diagonal. Position a small sunflower, a small sunflower center, and two leaves in the center of each of the resulting triangles. Glue and then appliqué the pieces in place. Repeat with the other pink 13¼ in. (33.7 cm) square. Cut the squares into triangles along the ironed creases, yielding four triangles.

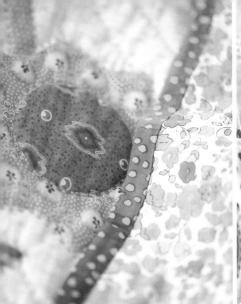

sewing and assembly

Quilt center

20. Referring to the quilt photograph, arrange the sunflower blocks, setting triangles, corner triangles, 15 in. (38.2 cm) sashing strips, and twenty-four of the 2 in. (5.1 cm) cornerstone squares on your design wall or work surface (see Tip on page 126). Rearrange the blocks until you are pleased with the color balance and placement.

21. Starting at the bottom right-hand corner, sew the blocks, sashing strips, and setting triangles together in diagonal rows. Press the seams toward the sashing.

22. Sew the remaining sashing strips and cornerstone squares together into strips for the sashing between the diagonal rows.

23. Sew a pieced sashing strip to the bottom of each row, matching the seams.

24. Sew the rows together. Sew the four corner triangles in place at the corners. Press the seams toward the sashing.

Inner border

25. Sew the remaining 2 in. (5.1 cm) striped sashing strips end-to-end to make one long strip. Measure your quilt top through the center in both directions. From the long strip, cut four pieces, each to this measurement.

26. Fold two of these border strips in half and mark the centers with pins. Mark the top and bottom edges of the quilt top in the same way. Matching the pins, the ends, and with right sides together, pin and then sew border strips to the top and bottom of the quilt top. Press the seams toward the border.

27. Sew a 2 in. (5.1 cm) cornerstone square to each end of the remaining two strips. In the same way, pin and then sew the pieced strips to the sides of the quilt top. Press the seams toward the border.

Outer border

28. Remove the selvages from the 10 in. (25.5 cm) pink strips. Sew the strips end-to-end to make one long strip, mixing the different pink fabrics. Press the seams.

29. Measure your quilt top through the center from top to bottom. From the long strip, cut two pieces, each to this measurement.

30. Fold the two border strips in half and mark the centers with pins. Mark the sides of the quilt top in the same way. Matching the pins, the ends, and with right sides together, pin and then sew the border strips to the sides of the quilt top. Press the seams toward the sashing.

31. Measure your quilt top through the center from side to side. From the long strip, cut two pieces, each to this measurement.

32. Fold the two border strips in half and mark the centers with pins. Mark the top and bottom of the quilt top in the same way. In the same way as in step 30, pin and then sew the strips to the top and bottom edges of the quilt top. Press the seams toward the inner border.

appliqué of outer border

33. Referring to the quilt photograph, position the eight small sunflowers and sunflower centers on the border. Each small sunflower lines up with a cornerstone in the quilt center, approximately 1 in. (2.5 cm) from the inner border. Position the two large corner sunflowers and sunflower centers, then the eight 22 in. (56 cm) stems, and the remaining leaves. Glue and then appliqué all the pieces in place.

backing, quilting, and binding

34. Cut the backing fabric crosswise into three 98 in. (2.5 m) lengths. Remove the selvages and sew the pieces together along the long edges to make the backing. Press the seams open and press the backing.

35. Layer the backing, batting (wadding), and quilt top, following the instructions on page 131.

36. Using dark pink Aurifil Mako' Ne 12 weight cotton thread, hand-quilt around the flowers, leaves, stems, and outer hearts following the instructions on pages 131–132. Outline-quilt around the inner hearts with blue thread.

37. Using masking tape, mark straight lines at random distances apart across the quilt. Using light pink thread, hand-quilt along these lines.

38. Bind the quilt, following the instructions on page 133.

smile, darn ya

You don't need to look far to see how I developed my design inspiration for this quilt. The sunflower was such a strong motif that I felt that distorting it too much would be a waste of a good thing. Instead I've chosen to blow it up and set it on a simple pieced background for maximum impact. I've called it Smile, Darn Ya because I felt there was something of a Little Orphan Annie feel about the vintage sheets and the blowsy flower.

Intended as a cheery throw, this huge sunflower was such fun to piece. I've been hoarding pieces of vintage cotton sheets for a while now, intending them for something special. The patterns of the 1960s and 1970s prints are so nostalgic, and I'm sure I had a few of the purple fabrics as pillowcases in my childhood! The combination of the vintage sheets and solid colors was a marriage made in heaven for a quilt combining old and new. As I don't like to use solid colors without texture, I decided that I would create my own texture with the quilting. The quilted squares within the squares add the touch of depth I felt the background was lacking.

If you have never appliquéd before, this is a great place to start. Large pieces make for quick projects, and if you choose fabrics with busy patterns for petals, your stitches won't show too much! If you are a veteran, then you will know what a quick and fun project this will be to create a cheery gift.

finished size

Large throw, 70½ in. (180 cm) square

Note All strips are cut across the width of the fabric from fold to selvage, and seams are stitched with right sides together using a ¼ in. (6 mm) seam allowance unless otherwise stated.

material requirements

- 18 in. (45.8 cm) each of at least eight different solid-color fabrics in pinks, blues, purples, and greens for background and cornerstones
- 12 in. (30.5 cm) striped fabric for inner border
- 36 in. (90 cm) text fabric for outer border
- Large scraps or fat quarters of vintage sheets (see page 124 or other print fabrics for sunflower center
- Nine different 7 x 10 in. (18 x 25.5 cm) yellow print pieces for sunflower petals
- Three different 8 x 11 in. (20.5 x 28 cm) green print pieces for leaves
- One fat quarter of green-and-white striped fabric for stem
- 26 in. (66 cm) solid pink fabric for binding
- 4½ yd (4.5 m) backing fabric
- 78 in. (2 m) square cotton batting (wadding)
- Two sheets of template plastic (see page 141 for templates)
- Pencil for tracing on template plastic

- Scissors for cutting template plastic
- Fabric scissors
- Hera marker for making bias strips
- Cotton thread for piecing
- Silver gel pen
- Appliqué glue
- Straw needles for appliqué
- Cotton thread to match appliqué fabrics
- Masking tape for marking quilting lines
- Crewel embroidery needles no. 9 for hand quilting
- Aurifil Mako' Ne 12 weight cotton to match solid-color fabrics for quilting
- Rotary cutter, mat, and ruler
- Sewing machine
- General sewing supplies

cutting

Note If you have not tried my method of needle-turn appliqué, read page 127 carefully before cutting or sewing anything. Even if you have done needle-turn appliqué before, read the project instructions carefully before starting.

From the template plastic, cut:
- One Template A (petal)
- One Template B (leaf)
- One Template C (quarter-circle)

Mark the templates with the appropriate letter on the right side.

From the solid-color fabrics, cut:
- Four 4½ in. (11.4 cm) strips from each fabric. Cross-cut the strips into 222 4½ in. (11.4 cm) squares. You will have more than enough fabric, which will enable you to mix the colors to your satisfaction.

From one solid-color fabric, cut:
- Four 1½ in. (3.8 cm) squares for cornerstones of inner border

From another solid-color fabric, cut:
- Four 4½ in. (11.4 cm) squares for cornerstones of outer border

From a few mixed solid-color fabrics, cut:
- Seven 2½ in. (6.3 cm) squares for outer borders

Tip I have used pieced squares of colored fabrics in the outer border, but if you prefer to leave these out, then make the outer border from just the text strips (and solid-color cornerstones) using the same method as for the inner border.

From striped fabric, cut:
- Seven 1½ in. (3.8 cm) strips for inner border

From text fabric, cut:
- One 2½ in. (6.3 cm) strip for outer border. Cross-cut the strip into fourteen 2½ in. (6.3 cm) squares.
- Seven 4½ in. (11.4 cm) strips for outer border. Cross-cut one strip into one 1½ x 4½ in. (6.3 x 11.4cm) rectangle, three 4½ in. (11.4 cm) squares, and one 7 x 4½ in. (17.8 x 11.4 cm) rectangle.

From yellow print fabric, cut:
- Nine Template A sunflower leaves, cutting ¼ in. (6mm) outside template

From green print fabric, cut:
- Three Template B leaves, cutting ¼ in. (6mm) outside template

From vintage-sheet fabrics, cut:
- Four 4½ in. (11.4 cm) squares for background
- Seven 2½ in. (6.3 cm) squares for outer border
- Selection of 1½ in. (3.8 cm) and 2½ in. (6.3 cm) strips for sunflower center. You will need enough strips to make seven 1½ x 20½ in. (3.8 x 52 cm) strips and seven 2½ x 20½ in. (6.3 x 52 cm) strips.

From green-and-white striped fabric, cut:
- 2 in. (5.1 cm) bias strips (see page 129) to equal 46 in. (117 cm)

From the solid pink fabric, cut:
- Eight 3 in. (7.6 cm) strips for binding

making the quilt
sewing and assembly

Background

1. On your design wall or work surface (see Tip on page 126), arrange the 4½ in. (11.4 cm) background squares (222 solid-color and three vintage-sheet squares) in rows, fifteen squares across and fifteen squares down. Mix the colors well. Remember that the squares at the right-hand top corner will be largely covered by the sunflower so don't put any of your favorite fabrics there.

2. When you are pleased with the layout, sew the squares in order into fifteen rows of fifteen, pressing the seams of adjacent rows in alternate directions. Matching the seams, sew the rows together to form the background square. Press the seams to one side, in the same direction.

Inner border

3. Measure your quilt top through the center in both directions—it should be 60½ in. (154.2 cm) square. If it is not, make a note of the measurement. Sew the seven 1½ in. (3.8 cm) striped strips end-to-end to make one long strip. Cut this strip into four pieces, each 60½ in. (154.2 cm) long, or the measurement of your quilt top.

4. Fold two of these border strips in half and mark the centers with pins. Mark the top and bottom edges of the quilt top in the same way. Matching the pins, the ends, and with right sides together, pin and then sew border strips to the top and bottom of the quilt top. Press the seams toward the border.

5. Sew a 1½ in. (3.8 cm) solid-color square to each end of the remaining two strips. In the same way, pin and then sew the pieced strips to the sides of the quilt top. Press the seams toward the border.

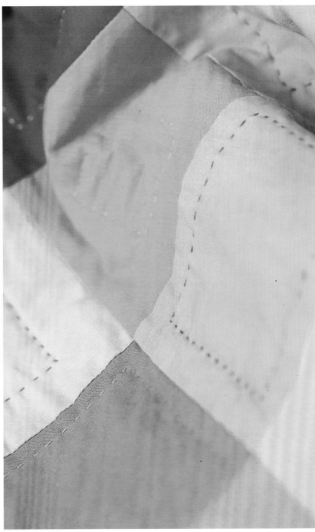

Outer border

6. Sew the seven 4½ in. (11.4 cm) text strips end-to-end to make one long strip.

7. Sew seven 2½ in. (6.3 cm) solid-color squares and seven 2½ in. (6.3 cm) text squares into pairs. Press the seams.

8. Sew seven 2½ in. (6.3 cm) sheet-fabric squares and seven 2½ in. (6.3 cm) text squares into pairs. Press the seams.

9. Measure your quilt top through the center in both directions—it should be 62½ in. (159.4 cm) square. If it is not, make a note of the measurement. From the long strip, cut four pieces 62½ in. (159.4 cm) long, or the measurement of your quilt top.

10. Sew three pieced pairs, one 2½ x 4½ in. (6.3 x 11.4 cm) text rectangle, two pieced pairs, one 4½ in. (11.4 cm) text square, and one pieced pair together in this order. Sew this to the end of one text border strip and trim the length to 62½ in. (159.4 cm) or the measurement of your quilt top. This is the top border.

11. Fold this pieced border strip and one text border strip in half and mark the centers with pins. Mark the top and bottom edges of the quilt top in the same way. Matching the pins and with right sides together, pin and sew the border strips to the top and bottom edges of the quilt top. Press the seams toward the border.

12. Sew four pieced pairs, one 4½ in. (11.4 cm) text square, two pieced pairs, one 4½ in. (11.4 cm) text square, one pieced pair, one 7 x 4½ in. (17.8 x 11.4 cm) text rectangle, and one pieced pair in this order. Sew this to the end of one text border strip and trim the length to 62½ in. (159.4 cm) or the measurement of your quilt. This is the left-hand side border.

13. Sew a 4½ in. (11.4 cm) solid-color square to each end of this border strip and to the remaining text border strip. In the same way as in step 11, pin and then sew the strips to the sides of the quilt top. Press the seams toward the border.

Sunflower center

14. Fold a piece of newspaper or similar into quarters. Place Template C on the folded corner and trace around the outside curved edge. Unfold the paper template to reveal a full circle.

15. Sew the 1½ in. (3.8 cm) strips of sheet fabric together end-to-end to make seven strips at least 20½ in. (52 cm) long. Press the seams. Repeat with the 2½ in. (6.3 cm) strips. Sew the strips into rows of alternating widths, starting with a 1½ in. (3.8 cm) strip. Press all the seams toward the 1½ in. (3.8 cm) strips. The piece does not have to be an accurate square.

16. Pin the paper circle template to the right side of the pieced square, and trace around the edge of the circle using the silver gel pen. Remove the template and cut out the pieced fabric ¼ in. (6 mm) outside the silver gel line.

Appliqué

17. Make a bias strip for the stem, following the instructions on page 129.

18. Arrange the sunflower stem, petals, and leaves on the pieced background, using the quilt photograph and the background squares as a guide. The petals and the end of the green stem should be completely underneath the sunflower, and the end of the leaves should be underneath the stem. Note that the sunflower, leaves, and stem extend into the borders.

19. Carefully lift the edges of the appliqué and put small dots of glue on the appliqué fabrics without moving them out of place. To ensure you can still turn the seam allowance under, avoid putting the glue too close to the edges.

20. When the glue has dried (about two minutes) finger-press around the gel pen line of a yellow petal. Thread a straw needle with thread to match the petal fabric, and knot the end of the thread.

21. Following the instructions on pages 127–128, appliqué around the outside of the shape. In the same way, appliqué the petals, leaves, and bias stem to the background fabric. Appliqué the sunflower center in place.

22. When the appliqué is complete, turn the quilt top over to the back and carefully cut the background fabric away from behind the sunflower center, leaves, and petals, ¼ in. (6 mm) from the stitching line, to reduce bulk.

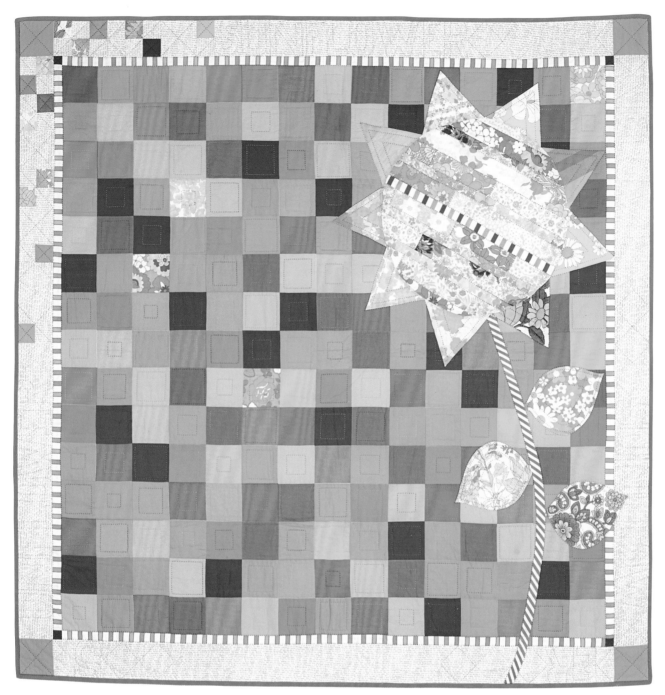

backing, quilting, and binding

23. Cut the backing fabric in half crosswise into two 78 in. (2 m) pieces. Remove the selvages and sew the pieces together along the long edges. Press the seam open and press the backing.

24. Layer the backing, batting (wadding), and quilt top, following the instructions on page 131.

25. Using masking tape, mark squares of different sizes within each background square. Use Aurifil Mako' Ne 12 weight cotton thread in various colors to hand-quilt the square shapes following the instructions on pages 131–132. Quilt along the strips in the sunflower center. Quilt around the outside of the sunflower, stem, and leaves. Using the shapes as guides, outline-quilt on the appliquéd petals and leaves. Quilt the word "SUNFLOWER" several times in the outer border and then fill the rest of the border with diagonal quilting lines.

26. Bind the quilt, following the instructions on page 133.

Centennial Quilt
Possibly Gertrude Knappenberger (dates unknown)
Possibly Emmaus, Pennsylvania
1876
Cotton with cotton embroidery
82½ x 74½"
Collection American Folk Art Museum, New York
Gift of Rhea Goodman, 1979.9.1

Centenary
Sarah's direct interpretation

In 1876, the United States of America celebrated its one-hundredth birthday as a nation. The country was becoming more and more populated and was on its way to becoming the major manufacturing force of the world.

There are many quilts in existence that were made to commemorate the Centennial. Some are made using the souvenir bandannas and scarves that were printed especially to celebrate the event. Although these quilts are not particularly elaborately pieced or beautifully quilted, they set themselves in history so squarely that they must be appreciated as wonderful artifacts.

Similarly seeking to commemorate their nation's birthday, other quilters made quilts of their own design. The quilt opposite, dated 1876, proudly announces itself in

centennial quilts

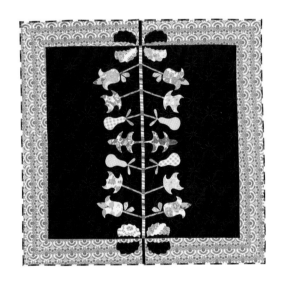

Mirror Image
Sarah's modern reinterpretation

the border as "CENTENNIAL" and clearly was made to honor this national event.

Dating quilts so proudly and visibly is seen fairly often in old quilts, but it is a tradition that seems to have died out in recent times. I like my quilts to have a sense of nostalgia and so I have proudly included the date my quilt was made in my direct interpretation, Centenary!

There is little doubt about the Pennsylvania German origin of this antique quilt. The baskets, stars, birds, tulips, and hearts are all designs that are found widely in quilts of the same origin. These images have been interpreted to have meaning and symbolism—the baskets, for example, are taken to mean plenty and abundance, much like a cornucopia. Tulips can be symbols of purity, and hearts, of course, of love and marriage. Whether the maker of the quilt, G. Knappenberger, who has displayed her name so proudly and prominently in the borders, meant to convey this meaning we cannot know.

finished size

Double-bed size quilt, 75½ in. (191.8 cm) wide
x 92 in. (235 cm) long

Note All strips are cut across the width of the
fabric from fold to selvage, and seams are
stitched with right sides together using a ¼ in.
(6 mm) seam allowance unless otherwise stated.

centenary

This quilt is a labor of love. The original is so detailed that I decided to
simplify things a little, otherwise it would have warranted a book of its
own! As a result, I opted to appliqué all the pieced blocks except the
center star, and to leave off the very detailed borders in favor of a lush
cream floral. The result still has the busy-ness of the original, without all
the work. Never fear, though—I used those wonderful shapes that were
left out, in the modern quilt that follows. Waste not, want not!

material requirements

Note This is a scrap quilt. There are many different fabrics used in
the blocks (including multiple shades of particular colors such as navy
or pink) and the material requirements reflect this and are approximate.
Feel free to substitute pieces from your stash where appropriate for
each block.

- 3¼ yd (3 m) natural linen for background
- 2 in. (6 cm) navy fabric for Template A pieces in center star
- 4 in. (11 cm) navy fabric for numbers of 2015
- 8 in. (21 cm) navy fabric for center star points
- Scraps of navy fabrics for Block 3 birds in first border
- 10 in. (26 cm) navy fabric for corner heart triangles in first border
- 12 in. (31 cm) each of two navy fabrics for Blocks 4 and 5
  (Templates Q and S) in first border
- 18 in. (46 cm) green fabric with small polka-dots for stems and leaves,
  four Template E pieces in center star, and Template U pieces in corner
  heart blocks
- Scraps of different blue, pink, and teal fabrics for Block 1 appliqué
  (Templates A–E) in first border and alternate Block 2 tulips
- One fat quarter of deep purple fabric for tulip blocks in center star
- 4 in. (11 cm) salmon pink fabric for tulip blocks in center star
- 20 in. (51 cm) hot pink graphic-print fabric for setting triangles
  and star points
- 8 in. (21 cm) dark purple fabric for Block 2 tulips in first border
- 8 in. (21 cm) hot pink fabric for Block 2 tulips in first border
- Scraps of yellow fabrics for Block 3 birds in first border
- 4 in. (11 cm) yellow fabric for Block 4 flowers in first border
- 16 in. (41 cm) light purple fabric for Block 3 baskets in first border
- 8 in. (21 cm) aqua fabric for corner heart triangles in first border
- 1⅓ yd (1.3 m) green fabric with large polka-dots for setting triangles
  and zigzag border
- One fat quarter each of four pink fabrics for outer border corners
- 3 yd (2.8 m) large floral print fabric for outer border
- 32 in. (82 cm) navy-and-white fabric for the binding
- 5⅔ yd (5.2 m) backing fabric
- 83 x 100 in. (211 x 254 cm) piece cotton batting (wadding)
- Cotton thread for piecing
- Eight sheets of template plastic (see page 149–153 for templates)
- Pencil for tracing on template plastic
- Scissors for cutting template plastic
- Fabric scissors
- Hera marker for making bias strips
- Silver gel pen
- Appliqué glue
- Straw needles for appliqué
- Cotton thread to match appliqué fabrics
- Small, sharp scissors for trimming appliqué
- Small piece of thin cardboard (a cereal box is ideal)
- Aluminum foil
- Rotary cutter, mat, and ruler
- Sewing machine
- General sewing supplies

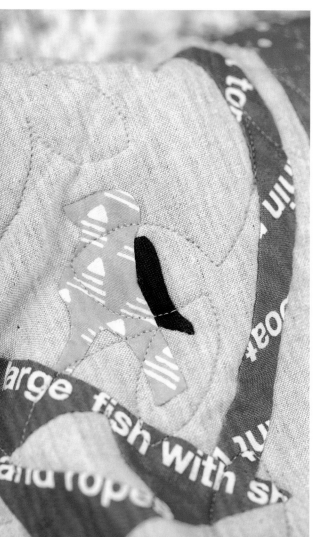

cutting

From the template plastic, cut:
- One each of Templates A–V. Mark the templates with the appropriate letter on the right side.
- Template W. This is a quarter-template, so trace the template four times to make a full template, ensuring that the sections meet where marked.
- One each of the number templates (provided for 2015)

From the natural linen, cut:
- One 6½ in. (16.5 cm) strip. Cross-cut this strip into four squares for corner tulip squares for center star.
- One 14 in. (35.6 cm) strip. Cross-cut this strip into one square. This is for the setting triangles for center star, but don't cut the triangles yet.
- Two 2⅜ in. (6 cm) strips. Cross-cut these strips into twenty-eight squares. Cross-cut these squares on one diagonal into fifty-six half-square triangles for star points.
- Three 9½ in. (24.1 cm) strips. Cross-cut these strips into twelve squares for appliqué blocks in first border.
- One 13¼ in. (33.7 cm) strip. Cross-cut this strip into two squares. These are for the corner heart triangles in first border, but don't cut the triangles yet.
- Four 2⅞ in. (7.3 cm) strips. Cross-cut these strips into fifty squares. Cross-cut these squares on one diagonal into one hundred half-square triangles for zigzag border.
- Two 14½ in. (36.8 cm) strips. Cross-cut these strips into four squares for outer border corners.
- One 10½ in. (26.7 cm) square for center of star
- Four 2 in. (5.1 cm) squares for center star points
- One 3⅜ in. (8.6 cm) square. Cross-cut this square on both diagonals into four quarter-square triangles for center star points.

From the green fabric with small polka-dots, cut:
- Two 1 in. (2.5 cm) strip. Cross-cut these strips into six 5 in. (12.7 cm) lengths for tulip stems in star corners and tulip setting triangles, and four 9 in. (22.9 cm) strips for Block 2 in first border.

From the navy star-point fabric, cut:
- Three 2⅜ in. (6 cm) strips. Cross-cut these strips into thirty-six squares. Cross-cut these squares on one diagonal into seventy-two half-square triangles for star points.

From the hot pink graphic-print fabric, cut:
- One 4⅞ in. (12.4 cm) strip. Cross-cut this strip into four squares. Cross-cut these squares on one diagonal into eight half-square triangles for star points.
- One 13½ in. (34.3 cm) strip. Cross-cut this strip into two squares. Cross-cut these squares on both diagonals into eight quarter-square triangles for setting triangles in first border.

From the light purple fabric, cut:
- Two 1 in. (2.5 cm) bias strips for basket handles in Block 3 in first border (but cut these strips only after you have cut two Template N—see opposite)

From the green fabric with large polka-dots, cut:
- One 13½ in. (34.3 cm) strip. Cross-cut this strip into two squares. Cross-cut these squares on both diagonals into eight quarter-square triangles for setting triangles in first border.
- Four 8½ in. (21.6 cm) strips. Cross-cut these strips into fifty 8½ x 2½ in. (21.6 x 6.3 cm) rectangles for zigzag border.

From the floral border fabric, cut:
- Seven 14½ in. (36.8 cm) strips for outer border

From the navy and white fabric, cut:
- Ten 3 in. (7.6 cm) strips for binding

cutting the appliqué fabrics

Note: If you have not tried my method of needle-turn appliqué, read page 127 carefully before cutting or sewing anything. Even if you have done needle-turn appliqué before, read the project instructions carefully before starting.

Using Template A, cut:
• Four in navy for Block 1 in center star
• Four in pink scraps for Block 1 in first border

Using Template B, cut:
• Four in medium blue for Block 1 in center star
• Four in pink scraps for Block 1 in first border

Using Template C, cut:
• One in navy for Block 1 in center star
• One in pink for Block 1 in first border

Using Template D, cut:
• One in pink for Block 1 in center star
• One in teal for Block 1 in first border

Using Template E, cut:
• Four in green fabric with small polka-dots for Block 1 in center star
• Four in teal for Block 1 in first border

Using Template F, cut:
• Six in salmon fabric for tulip blocks in center star

Using Template G, cut:
• Six in deep purple fabric for tulip blocks in center star
• Six in deep purple fabric using Template G reverse for tulip blocks in center star

Using Template H, cut:
• Six in green fabric with small polka-dots for tulip blocks in center star
• Six in green fabric with small polka-dots using Template H reverse for tulip blocks in center star

Using Template I, cut:
• Six in dark purple fabric for side Block 2 in first border
• Six in pink fabric for side Block 2 in first border
• One in teal fabric for bottom Block 2 in first border
• Two in hot pink fabric for bottom Block 2 in first border

Using Template J, cut:
• Six in dark purple for side Block 2 in first border
• Six in pink for side Block 2 in first border
• One in hot pink for bottom Block 2 in first border
• Two in teal for bottom Block 2 in first border

Using Template K, cut:
• Fifteen in green fabric with small polka-dots for Block 2 in first border

Using Template L, cut:
• Five in green fabric with small polka-dots for Block 2 in the first border
• Five in green fabric with small polka-dots using Template L reverse for Block 2 in first border

Using Template M, cut:
• Five in green fabric with small polka-dots for Block 2 in first border
• Five in green fabric with small polka-dots using Template M reverse for Block 2 in first border

Using Template N, cut:
• Two in light purple for Block 3 in first border. Trace the triangle cut-outs also, and cut them out a scant ¼ in. (6 mm) inside the traced line.

Using Template O, cut:
• Two in yellow fabric for Block 3 in first border
• Two in yellow fabric using Template O reversed for Block 3 in first border

Using Template P, cut:
• Two in navy fabric for Block 3 in first border
• Two in navy fabric using Template P reversed for Block 3 in first border

Using Template Q, cut:
• Two in different navy fabrics for Block 4 in first border

Using Template R, cut:
• Eight in yellow fabric for Block 4 in first border

Using Template S, cut:
• Two in different navy fabrics for Block 5 in first border

Using Template T, cut:
• Four in navy for corner heart triangles in first border

Using Template U, cut:
• Eight in green fabric with small polka-dots for corner heart triangles in first border

Using Template V, cut:
• Four in aqua for corner heart triangles in first border

Using Template W, cut:
• Four in different pink fabrics for corner blocks in outside border

Using the number templates, cut:
• Two of each number in navy fabric

making the quilt

center star

Block 1 appliqué

1. Make the navy Template C piece and the pink Template C piece into perfect circles using the foil technique on page 128. Set the pink circle aside to use later in Block 1 of the first border.

2. Fold and then finger-press the 10½ in. (26.7 cm) linen square into quarters on the straight grain of the fabric. Refold and then press the square into quarters on the diagonal.

3. Working on your design wall or work surface (see Tip on page 126), arrange on the linen square the appliqué pieces A, B, C, D, and E for Block 1, using the pressed lines and the quilt photograph as guides (see Diagram 1). When everything is in place, carefully lift the edges of the appliqué and put small dots of glue onto the appliqué fabrics without moving them out of place. To ensure

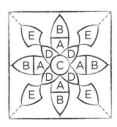

diagram 1

you can still turn the seam allowance under, do not put the glue too close to the edges. Always start with the underneath piece. Following the instructions on pages 127–128, appliqué the pieces in place. Press the block.

diagram 2

diagram 3

diagram 4

diagram 5

diagram 6

diagram 7

Corner tulip blocks appliqué

4. Following the instructions on page 129 step 3, mark the creases on the six small-polka-dotted green fabric strips for tulip stems. (Note that these strips have been cut on the straight grain, not on the bias.)

5. Fold and then finger-press a 6½ in. (16.5 cm) linen square in half on one diagonal. Place one of the stem strips along the diagonal crease. Arrange one each of the appliqué pieces F, G, G-reversed, H, and H-reversed for the tulip on the square (see Diagram 2). Glue and then appliqué in place. Press the block. Make four corner tulip blocks for the center star.

2015 and tulip setting triangles appliqué

6. Fold and then press the 14 in. (35.6 cm) linen square into quarters on the diagonals. Arrange the remaining creased strips and F, G, G-reversed, H, and H-reversed appliqué pieces for two tulips on the square, noting that the stems run from the center of the block (see Diagram 3). Do not place any appliqué pieces too close to the folds or the edges of the block or you may lose them in a seam or when trimming the star square later.

7. Arrange the two sets of numbers on the other two quarters of the square. Glue and then appliqué all the pieces in place. Press the block. Cut the square into quarters along the diagonal folds, forming the four setting triangles.

Sewing and assembly

8. Sew linen and navy half-square triangles in pairs along the diagonal edges, to make fifty-six half-square triangle pairs. Press the seams toward the navy blue fabric and trim the "ears."

9. Sew three of these half-square triangle pairs together with the navy blue triangles facing to the right. Sew a single navy half-square triangle to the top of this unit. Press the seams toward the navy fabric. Sew this unit to the right-hand side of one of the corner tulip squares (see Diagram 4). Press the seam toward the tulip block.

10. Sew three half-square triangle pairs together with the navy blue triangles facing to the left. Sew a single navy blue triangle to the top of this unit and a 2 in. (5.1 cm) linen square to the bottom. Press the seams toward the navy blue fabric. Sew this unit to the bottom of one of the corner tulip squares (see Diagram 5). Press the seam toward the tulip block. Make four of these.

11. Sew four half-square triangle pairs together with the navy blue triangles facing to the left. Sew a single navy blue triangle to the top of this unit. Press the seams toward the navy blue fabric. Sew a hot pink graphic-print half-square triangle to the unit and press the seam toward the pink fabric (see Diagram 6). Take care when pressing, as this is a bias edge. Make four of these.

12. Sew four half-square triangle pairs together with the navy blue triangles facing to the right. Sew a single navy blue triangle to the top of this unit and a linen quarter-square triangle to the bottom, with the bias edge against the navy blue.

Press the seams toward the navy blue fabric. Sew this strip to a pink graphic-print half-square triangle and press toward the pink fabric (see Diagram 7). Make four of these.

13. Stitch the star point that does not have a quarter-square linen triangle at the bottom to the left-hand side of one of the 2015 setting triangles. Press the seam carefully toward the setting triangle, remembering that this is a bias edge. This piece is shorter than the setting-triangle edge, so match the right-angled corners of the 2015 setting triangle and the star point as shown (see Diagram 8). Leave the seam open where shown at the dots.

14. Sew the other star point to the other side of the same setting triangle, again leaving the seam open at the dots, and aligning the quarter-square triangle with the navy blue triangle on the opposite strip (see Diagram 9). Press the seam toward the setting triangle. Make four of these—two with 2015 appliqué and two with tulip appliqué.

15. Sew one of the 2015 units to the top and the other to the bottom of the center star (see Diagram 10).

16. Sew a corner tulip square to the straight edge of the left-hand side of one of the tulip setting triangles, only sewing to the star points, not to the linen setting triangle (see Diagram 11).

17. Complete the seam by sewing the piece to the linen triangle (see Diagram 12). In the same way, sew another tulip corner to the other side of the setting triangle. Make two of these setting triangle units.

18. Sew a setting triangle unit to each side of the star, taking care to match the seams, and closing the open seams as previously described. Press the star and trim the square, if needed.

first border

Block 1 appliqué
19. Referring to the quilt photograph on page 66 (in which Block 1 can be seen just above the center star), arrange the A, B, C, D, and E appliqué pieces for Block 1 on a 9½ in. (24.1 cm) linen square. Glue and then appliqué all the pieces in place. Press the block.

Block 2 appliqué
20. Following the instructions on page 129 step 3, mark the creases on the 1 x 9 in. (2.5 x 22.9 cm) strips of green fabric with small polka-dots that you cut for tulip stems (which are cut straight, not on the bias).

21. Fold and then press a 9½ in. (24.1 cm) linen square into quarters on the diagonals. Referring to the quilt photograph (in which Block 2 can be seen just below the center star) and the tulip block placement diagram on page 150, arrange the I, J, K, L, L-reversed, M, and M-reversed appliqué pieces for the first border's Block 2 on the square, using the diagonal folds as guides. The tips of the flowers should sit just over ¼ in. (6 mm) from the edge of the block so that they almost touch the seams when pieced into the quilt. Note the color placement—each Block 2 has the colors reversed on the top and the side tulips. The fifth block uses different colors and will sit at the bottom edge of the first border. Glue and then appliqué all the pieces in place. Press the block. Make five Block 2.

Block 3 appliqué
22. Fold and then press a 9½ in. (24.1 cm) linen square in half along one diagonal. Referring to the quilt photograph (in which one Block 3

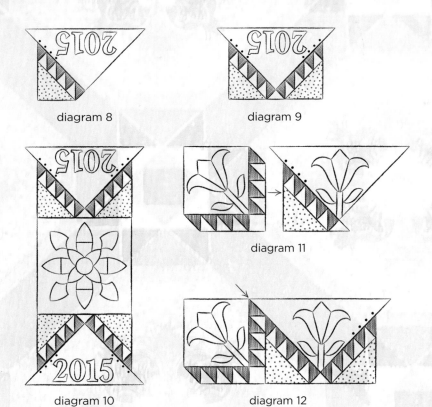
diagram 8
diagram 9
diagram 10
diagram 11
diagram 12

can be seen to the left of the center star, and the other to the right of the center star), arrange the N basket appliqué piece on the square, using this fold as a guide. Arrange the O and O-reversed birds along the edge of the basket and the P and P-reversed wings beneath them.

23. Referring to the instructions on page 129, make bias strips from the light purple strips and curve the basket handles in place. Glue and then appliqué all the pieces in place. Finger-press the seam allowance around the triangle shapes, pressing the fabric underneath the basket. Carefully reverse-appliqué (see page 153) around the triangles so that the linen shows through. Press the block. Make two Block 3.

Block 4 appliqué
24. Fold and then press a 9½ in. (24.1 cm) linen square into quarters along both diagonals. Referring to the quilt photograph (in which one Block 4 can be seen directly above the bottom left-hand corner heart triangle, and the other directly below the top right-hand corner heart triangle), arrange the Template Q

pieces so that the arms and points of the shape are along both diagonals, using the folds as guides. Glue the pieces in place. Position a Template R flower in each space between the arms, and glue. Appliqué all pieces. Press the block. Make two Block 4.

Block 5 appliqué
25. Fold and then press a 9½ in. (24.1 cm) linen square into quarters along both diagonals for Block 5. Referring to the quilt photograph (in which one Block 5 can be seen to the right of the top left-hand corner heart triangle, and the other to the left of the bottom right-hand corner heart triangle), arrange the Template S piece so that the arms and points of the shape are along both diagonals, using the folds as guides. Glue and then appliqué the pieces in place. Press the block. Make two Block 5.

Corner heart triangles appliqué
26. Make the green small-polka-dotted Template U pieces into perfect circles using the foil technique on page 128. Fold and then press a 13¼ in. (33.7 cm) linen square in half along one diagonal for

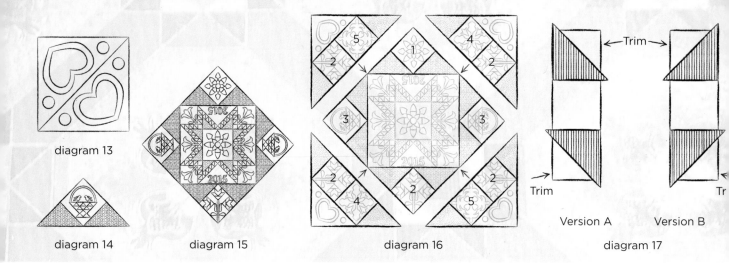

diagram 13

diagram 14

diagram 15

diagram 16

Version A

Version B

diagram 17

a corner block. Arrange a Template T and Template V heart and two Template U circles in each half of the square (see Diagram 13). Glue and then appliqué the pieces in place. Turn the block over to the back and carefully cut the background fabric and the Template T fabric away from behind the small heart, ¼ in. (6 mm) from the stitching line. Press the block. Make two squares. Cut the squares in half along the fold to make four corner heart triangles.

Sewing and assembly
27. Sew a green large-polka-dotted setting triangle to the two bottom edges of Block 1, of the two Block 3 baskets, and of the bottom Block 2, ensuring the blocks are correctly oriented (see Diagram 14 and the quilt photograph).

28. Again taking careful note of position and orientation, sew one of these units to the top of the center star and one to the bottom of the center star. Press the seams toward the center star, ensuring you do not stretch the bias edges. Sew the two basket units to opposite sides of the center star and press (see Diagram 15).

29. Sew the blocks for the corners of the quilt together and to the hot pink setting triangles, taking note of orientation and placement. Press the seams to one side. Sew a corner heart triangle to each of these four units, and press the seams to one

side. Sew one of these units to each side of the center star (see Diagram 16, in which the numbers indicate the blocks). Press the seams to one side.

zigzag border

30. Sew a 2⅞ in. (7.3 cm) linen triangle to each end of a 2½ x 8½ in. (6.3 x 21.6 cm) green large-polka-dotted strip, positioning the triangles so that the "ears" are ¼ in. (6 mm) over the edges of the strip each time. Make twenty-six with the triangles oriented as shown for version A and twenty-four as for version B (see Diagram 17). Trim the "ears," and then trim the green large-polka-dotted fabric from the corners and press the seams toward the linen triangles.

31. Join the pieced rectangles end-to-end into two strips of twenty-five rectangles each, matching the points of the linen triangles, and alternating the A and B units to form a zigzag.

32. Mark the centers of one strip and of the top of the quilt top with pins. Matching the pins and with right sides together, pin the border strip to the quilt top, pinning along the length of the border. Sew the top border in place. Press the seam toward the border. In the same way, pin and then sew the bottom border in place.

outer border

33. Fold and then finger-press a 14½ in. (36.8 cm) linen square into quarters along both diagonals. Referring to the photograph and using the folds as guides, arrange a Template W piece on the square. Glue and then appliqué in place. Make four corner blocks.

34. Sew the 14½ in. (36.8 cm) floral border strips end-to-end to make one long strip, removing the selvages.

35. Measure the quilt top through the center from top to bottom. From the long strip, cut two pieces to this measurement. Fold the two border strips in half and mark the centers with pins. Mark the sides of the quilt top in the same way. Matching pins, the ends, and with right sides together, pin and then sew the border strips to the left-hand and right-hand sides of the quilt top. Press the seams toward the borders.

36. Measure the quilt top through the center from side to side (not including the side outer borders). Add ½ in. (12 mm) for the seam allowances and then cut two pieces to this measurement from the long strip for the top and bottom borders. Pin and then sew a corner block to either end of these strips. Pin and then sew these borders to the top and bottom edges of the quilt top. Press the seams toward the borders.

backing, quilting, and binding

37. Cut the backing fabric crosswise into two 102 in. (2.6 m) pieces. Remove the selvages and sew the pieces together along the long edges to make the backing. Press the seam open and press the backing.

38. Layer the backing, batting (wadding), and quilt top, following the instructions on page 131. If you are going to have the quilt professionally machine-quilted, do not layer it.

39. Quilt as desired. Mine was professionally machine-quilted in a delicate leafy pattern.

40. Bind the quilt, following the instructions on page 133.

mirror image

The wonderful bottom border on the antique quilt inspired this design—it seemed too much of a good thing to waste! With its funky shapes and negative space, this quilt is fun and sparky. I used a combination of vintage sheets and feedsack fabrics for the appliqué and was lucky enough to find the perfect retro-look fabric for the border. This is a great quilt if you are a beginner to needleturn appliqué. The large, softly curved shapes lend themselves perfectly to an easy and enjoyable project.

finished size

Double-bed size topper or throw, 76½ in. (194.5 cm) square

Note All strips are cut across the width of the fabric from fold to selvage, and seams are stitched with right sides together using a ¼ in. (6 mm) seam allowance unless otherwise stated.

material requirements

- 6 in. (16 cm) green patterned fabric for large leaves
- 8 in. (21 cm) orange patterned fabric for bell-shaped flowers
- 12 in. (31 cm) blue patterned fabric for flower centers and double leaves
- 8 in. (21 cm) pink patterned fabric for small flowers
- 6 in. (16 cm) yellow patterned fabric for pear-shaped flowers
- 10 in. (26 cm) green fabric for thin stems, small fat leaves, and small thin leaves
- 4 in. (10 cm) multicolor striped fabric for main stem
- 3½ yd (3.2 m) solid navy fabric for background and large leaves
- 2 yd (2 m) floral print fabric for border
- 28 in. (2 m) navy striped fabric for binding
- 4¾ yd (4.4 m) backing fabric
- 85 in. (216 cm) square cotton batting (wadding)

- Cotton thread for piecing
- Five sheets of template plastic (see pages 138–139 for templates)
- Pencil for tracing on template plastic
- Scissors for cutting template plastic
- Fabric scissors
- Hera marker for making bias strips
- Silver gel pen
- Appliqué glue
- Straw needles for appliqué
- Cotton thread to match appliqué fabrics
- Small, sharp scissors for trimming appliqué
- Rotary cutter, mat, and ruler
- Sewing machine
- General sewing supplies

cutting

Note If you have not tried my method of needle-turn appliqué, read page 127 carefully before cutting or sewing anything. Even if you have done needle-turn appliqué before, read the project instructions carefully before starting.

From the template plastic, cut:
- One each of Templates A (large leaf), B (bell-shaped flower), C (flower center), D (small flower), E (pear-shaped flower), F (double leaf), G (small fat leaf), and H (small thin leaf). Mark the templates with the appropriate letter on the right side.

From the green patterned fabric, cut:
- Four Template A large leaves—two right way up and two reversed

From the orange patterned fabric, cut:
- Four Template B bell-shaped flowers

From the blue patterned fabric, cut:
- Four Template C flower centers
- Two Template F double leaves

From the pink patterned fabric, cut:
- Four Template D small flowers

From the yellow patterned fabric, cut:
- Four Template E pear-shaped flowers

From the green fabric, cut:
- Three 1 in. (2.5 cm) strips for the thin stems
- Eight Template G small fat leaves
- Eight Template H small thin leaves

From the solid navy fabric, cut:
- Two 60½ in. (153.7 cm) pieces for background
- One 1½ in. (3.8 cm) strip for main stem on border
- Four Template A large leaves for border

From the floral print fabric, cut:
- Eight 8½ in. (21.6 cm) strips for border

From the multicolor striped fabric, cut:
- Two 1½ in. (3.8 cm) strips for main stem

From the navy striped fabric, cut:
- Nine 3 in. (7.6 cm) strips for the binding

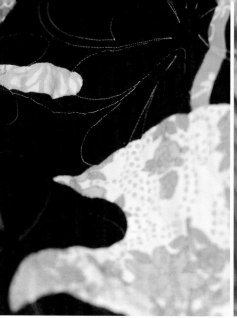

borders

10. Sew two 8½ in. (21.6 cm) floral print border strips end-to-end to make one long strip. Trim to measure 77 in. (195.7 cm) long, matching the pattern at the seam if the fabric allows, and ensuring the seam is exactly at the center of the strip. Make four of these strips.

11. On two of the strips, glue and then appliqué the navy blue strip exactly over the center seam. Referring to the quilt photograph for placement, place a navy blue Template A large leaf on each side of the stem, and then glue and appliqué in place.

12. Use pins to mark the center of the appliqué strip on the top and bottom borders, and the center of the top and bottom of the quilt, taking care to match the stems. The borders will be wider than the quilt top. Matching the pins, the ends, and with right sides together, pin the border strips to the quilt top, pinning along the length of the border. Sew the borders in place, starting and finishing ¼ in. (6 mm) from the ends. Press the seams toward the borders.

13. In the same way, pin and then sew the side borders to the quilt top, again starting and finishing ¼ in. (6 mm) from the ends.

14. Miter the corners of the borders, following the instructions on page 130. Press the seams to one side.

making the quilt
sewing and assembly of background

1. Remove the selvages from the two navy background pieces and sew the pieces together along the middle seam to make the background. Press the seam allowance open. Trim the whole piece to measure 60½ in. (153.7 cm) square, with the seam running vertically along the center.

2. Sew the multicolor striped 1½ in. (3.8 cm) strips end-to-end to make one long strip, and trim to 60½ in. (153.7 cm) long. Following the instructions on page 129 step 3, mark the creases on it (note that this strip is cut straight, not on the bias).

3. In the same way, make four 10 in.- (25.4 cm-) long stems from each of the three 1 in.- (2.5 cm-) wide green strips, so you have twelve in total, and make two 8½ in.- (21.6 cm-) long strips from the 1½ in.- (3.8 cm-) wide solid navy strip.

4. Fold and then press the 60½ in. (153.7 cm) background piece in half so the crease runs horizontally from left side to right side.

appliqué of background

5. Working on your design wall or work surface (see Tip on page 126), place the multicolor striped strip from step 2 exactly over the vertical center seam on the background piece, from edge to edge. Secure the strip in place with a few drops of glue.

6. Center the two blue Template F double leaves along the creased horizontal line and then glue in place.

7. Referring to the quilt photograph for positioning, place the twelve thin green stems along the length of the striped main stem at an angle, about 7 in. (18 cm) apart from each other. Glue the thin stems in place.

8. Again referring to the quilt photograph, arrange the flowers and leaves on the thin stems. When everything is in place, carefully lift the edges of the appliqué and put small dots of glue onto the appliqué fabrics without moving them out of place. To ensure you can still turn the seam allowance under, do not put the glue too close to the edges.

9. Following the instructions on pages 127–128, appliqué the pieces in place. Press the appliqué.

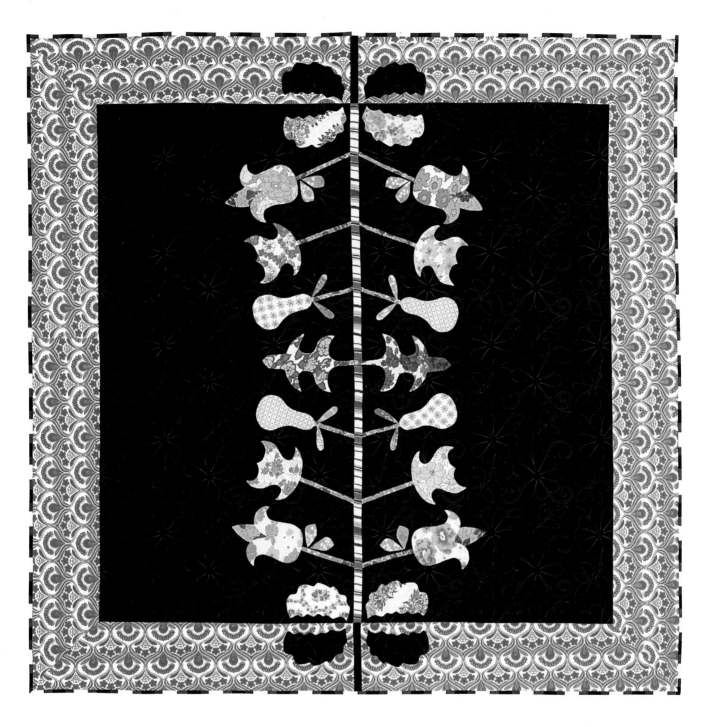

backing, quilting, and binding

15. Cut the backing fabric crosswise into two 85 in. (2.2 m) pieces. Remove the selvages and sew the pieces together along the long edges to make the backing. Press the seam open and press the backing.

16. Layer the backing, batting (wadding), and quilt top, following the instructions on page 131. If you are going to have the quilt professionally machine-quilted, do not layer it.

17. Quilt as desired. Mine was professionally machine-quilted in a funky floral design.

18. Bind the quilt, following the instructions on page 133.

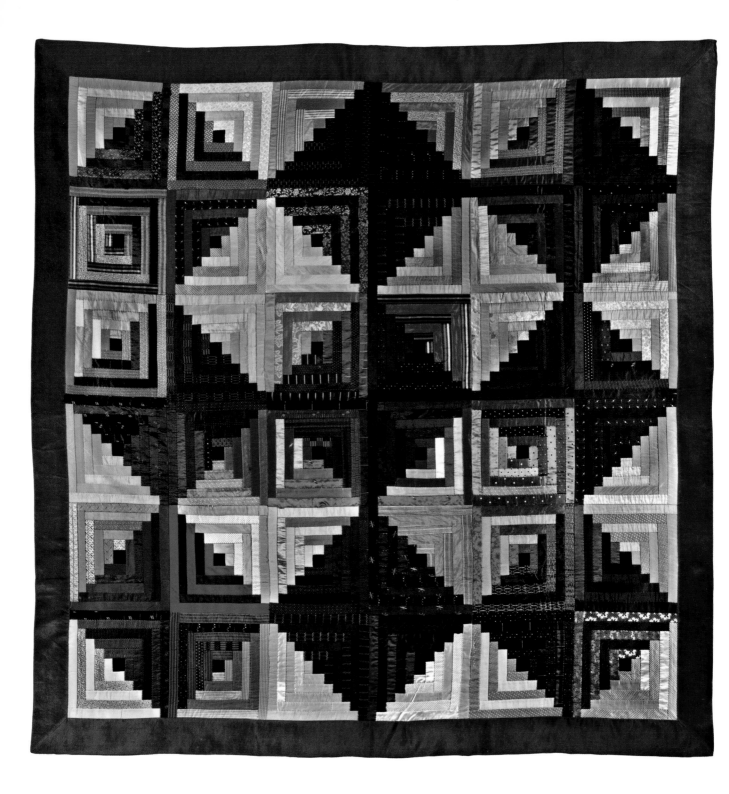

Log Cabin Throw, Light-and-Dark Variation
Harriet Rutter Eagleson (1855–1950)
New York City
1875–1880
Silk and cotton
57³⁄₄ x 57³⁄₄"
Collection American Folk Art Museum, New York
Gift of Miss Jessica R. Eagleson, 1979.18.1
Photo by Gavin Ashworth

Liberty Belle
Sarah's direct interpretation

The Log Cabin is one of the best-loved and most recognized of quilt blocks. Although most quilters assume this block originated from an American log cabin during early settlement, in fact the pattern has been found in old English quilts of the early 1800s and even on a mummified Ancient Egyptian cat!

Most antique Log Cabin quilts were constructed by sewing strips of fabric to a foundation. At the time, this was a new and innovative method of construction. Previously, quilts were usually made using either English paper piecing or a simple running stitch. Quilts made using this method were often very heavy because of the extra foundation layer and the popular use of materials such as velvet, wool, satin, and decorative ribbons. There was no need for batting

log cabin quilts

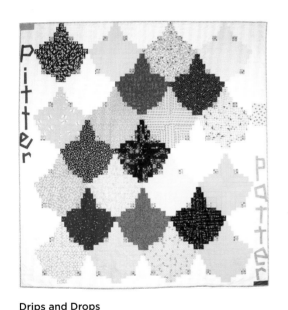

Drips and Drops
Sarah's modern reinterpretation

(wadding) and the quilts were usually tied instead of quilted.

Over the years, many block and setting variations of the Log Cabin emerged. These were given their own names, such as Barn Raising, Windmill Blades, Pineapple, Courthouse Steps, and Sunshine and Shadows.

Log Cabin quilts were some of the first quilts thought to be used to convey a message. A yellow center block represented a candle in the window, or a welcoming light; a red center block symbolized the hearth of your home. Legend has it that a Log Cabin quilt with a black center block was hung on the washing line to signal a stop on the Underground Railroad, an escape route for slaves from the American South. Although most historians now believe this to be an urban myth, it's certainly a poignant story.

Whatever its origin or meaning, the Log Cabin block is still a source of fascination to modern quilters. The endless design possibilities of light and dark, print and color placement, length and width of strips, and the size of the center square can produce graphic and unexpected results.

My interpretations of Harriet Rutter Eagleson's Log Cabin Throw feature a traditional mix of light and dark fabrics in Liberty Belle, and variations in the width and length of strips to create a raindrop shape in Drips and Drops.

liberty belle

The striking solid colors and satins of the original quilt make a wonderfully strong design but I wanted to achieve the pattern with prints. All the fabrics in this quilt are lawns from Liberty of London. I began with a pile of fabrics I loved, separated them into light and dark, and then culled any I felt were reading as medium.

I have used a wide range of different prints here. If you'd like your quilt to look as scrappy as mine, you will need less yardage of more prints than specified in the material requirements. There are five light and five dark fabrics in each of the thirty-six blocks, so potentially 360 different light and dark fabrics! Try swapping some prints with friends to achieve a bigger selection.

finished size

Large throw, or quilt for end of a double bed, 72½ in. (184.6 cm) square

Note All strips are cut across the width of the fabric from fold to selvage, and seams are stitched with right sides together using a ¼ in. (6 mm) seam allowance unless otherwise stated.

Tip This quilt can easily be made larger or smaller by changing the number of blocks and rows. To make a double bed quilt, 55 x 88 in. (142 x 224 cm), make eight rows of four blocks with a 6 in. (15 cm) border at the sides to make the quilt wide enough. To make a queen bed-size (UK: king-size) quilt, 94 in. (239 cm) square, make eight rows of eight blocks plus a 3 in. (7.5 cm) border. Adjust the material requirements accordingly.

material requirements

- 4 in. (10 cm) feature print for center of blocks (see note)
- 6 in. (15 cm) each of twenty different light print fabrics
- 6 in. (15 cm) each of twenty different dark print fabrics
- 32 in. (82 cm) dark floral fabric for border
- 26 in. (66 cm) floral print fabric for binding
- 4½ yd (4.2 m) backing fabric
- 79 in. (2 m) square cotton batting (wadding)
- Cotton thread for piecing
- Rotary cutter, mat, and ruler
- Sewing machine
- General sewing supplies

Note I fussy-cut the center fabric. In order to get thirty-six fussy-cut blocks you may need more fabric than specified, depending on the print. I used 12 in. (31 cm) of feature print to cut enough houses in exactly the right place. Also bear in mind that if you are using Liberty of London lawns, you will need a little less fabric than stated here because they are wider than regular patchwork fabric. Finally, to keep your Log Cabins flat, see the important Tip on page 81 of Drips and Drops.

cutting

From the feature print, cut:
- Thirty-six 1⅝ in. (4.1 cm) squares

From the light print fabrics, cut:
- 1⅝ in. (4.1 cm) strips. Choose five of these strips for each block and cross-cut the strips into rectangles of these lengths:
Fabric 1—1⅝ in. (4.1 cm) and 2⅝ in. (6.7 cm)
Fabric 2—3⅝ in. (9.2 cm) and 4⅝ in. (11.7 cm)
Fabric 3—5⅝ in. (14.3 cm) and 6⅝ in. (16.8 cm)
Fabric 4—7⅝ in. (19.4 cm) and 8⅝ in. (21.9 cm)
Fabric 5—9⅝ in. (24.5 cm) and 10⅝ in. (27 cm)

From the dark print fabrics, cut:
- 1⅝ in. (4.1 cm) strips. Choose five of these strips for each block and cross-cut the strips into rectangles of these lengths:
Fabric 1—2⅝ in. (6.7 cm) and 3⅝ in. (9.2 cm)
Fabric 2—4⅝ in. (11.7 cm) and 5⅝ in. (14.3 cm)
Fabric 3—6⅝ in. (16.8 cm) and 7⅝ in. (19.4 cm)
Fabric 4—8⅝ in. (21.9 cm) and 9⅝ in. (24.5 cm)
Fabric 5—10⅝ in. (27 cm) and 11⅝ in. (29.6 cm)

Note There are thirty-six blocks so you will need to cut these light and dark strips for each block, for a total of thirty six sets of strips.

From the dark floral fabric, cut:
- Eight 3½ in. (8.9 cm) strips for border

From the floral print fabric, cut:
- Eight 3 in. (7.6 cm) strips for binding

diagram 1

diagram 2

diagram 3

diagram 4

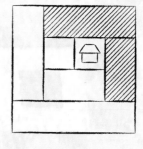
diagram 5

making the quilt

sewing

1. Sew a light 1⅝ in. (4.1 cm) fabric 1 square to the left-hand side of the center square and then press (see Diagram 1).

2. Sew a light 2⅝ in. (6.7 cm) fabric 1 rectangle to the bottom of the unit and then press. Trim the unit to measure 2½ in. (6.3 cm) square (see Diagram 2).

3. Sew a dark 2⅝ in. (6.7 cm) fabric 1 rectangle to the right-hand side of the unit and then press (see Diagram 3).

4. Sew a dark 3⅝ in. (9.2 cm) fabric 1 rectangle to the top of the unit and then press. Trim the unit to measure 3½ in. (8.9 cm) square (see Diagram 4).

5. In the same way, sew a light 3⅝ in. (9.2 cm) fabric 2 rectangle to the left-hand side of the unit and then a light 4⅝ in. (11.7 cm) fabric 2 rectangle to the bottom of the unit and press. Trim the unit to measure 4½ in. (11.2 cm) square (see Diagram 5).

6. Continue sewing the block in this way, trimming the unit after every round of light or dark is added. The finished block will have ten light and ten dark pieces (plus the feature-print center). Trim the block to measure 11½ in. (29.2 cm) square.

7. Make thirty-six blocks.

assembly

8. Referring to the quilt photograph, arrange the quilt blocks on your design wall or work surface (see Tip on page 126) in six rows of six blocks. Note that the blocks are rotated a quarter-turn to form the light and dark diamonds in the design. When you are pleased with the arrangement, sew the blocks together into rows, and press the seams of each alternate row in opposite directions.

9. Sew the six rows together and press the seams.

border

10. Remove the selvages from the 3½ in. (8.9 cm) dark floral strips. Sew the strips end-to-end to make one long strip.

11. Measure the quilt top through the center from top to bottom. It should be 66½ in. (168.9 cm). From the long strip, cut two pieces to this measurement.

12. Fold the two border strips in half and mark the centers with pins. Mark the sides of the quilt top in the same way. Matching pins, the ends, and with right sides together, pin and then sew border strips to the sides of the quilt top. Press the seams toward the borders.

13. Measure the quilt top through the center from side to side. From the remaining long strip, cut two pieces to this measurement. Fold the strips in half and mark the centers with pins. Mark the top and bottom of the quilt top in the same way. Matching pins and with right sides together, pin and then sew border strips to the top and bottom of the quilt top. Press the seams toward the borders.

backing, quilting, and binding

14. Cut the backing fabric into two 81 in. (206 cm) pieces. Remove the selvages and sew the pieces together along the long edges to make the backing. Press the seam open and press the backing.

15. If you are going to do the quilting yourself, layer the backing, batting (wadding), and quilt top, following the instructions on page 131. If you are going to have the quilt professionally machine-quilted, do not layer it.

16. Quilt as desired. Mine was professionally machine-quilted in an all-over floral design.

17. Bind the quilt, following the instructions on page 133.

drips and drops

Log Cabins are so versatile. Changing the width and length of the strips and the size of the center starting block can change the perspective and the scope of the design without having to change the fundamental construction of the block.

In this quilt I have halved the width of some of the strips to create an off-center Log Cabin, shaped like a raindrop. If you want your quilt to look more watery, replace the white with several different light and medium blues.

finished size

King-size (UK: superking-size) bed quilt, 100½ in. (255.8 cm) wide x 104½ in. (266 cm) long

Note All strips are cut across the width of the fabric from fold to selvage, and seams are stitched with right sides together using a ¼ in. (6 mm) seam allowance unless otherwise stated.

Tip This quilt can be made smaller by changing the number of blocks and rows. To make a throw quilt, make three dark drops across and three down. You will need to adjust the material requirements accordingly.

material requirements

- 12 in. (30.5 cm) pink fabric for block centers
- 4½ yd (4.2 m) white fabric
- 13 in. (33 cm) each of eight different dark blue fabrics
- 13 in. (33 cm) each of fourteen different light blue fabrics
- 12 in. (30.5 cm) extra dark blue fabric for letters in border
- 12 in. (30.5 cm) extra light blue fabric for letters in border
- 1 yd. (1 m) light blue fabric for binding
- 9 yd. (8.3 m) backing fabric
- 108 x 112 in. (275 x 285 cm) piece cotton batting (wadding)
- Cotton thread for piecing
- Rotary cutter, mat, and ruler
- Sewing machine
- General sewing supplies

cutting

From the pink fabric, cut:
- Four 2⅝ in. (6.7 cm) strips. Cross-cut these strips into sixty-four 2⅝ in. (6.7 cm) squares.

From the white fabric, cut:
- Twenty-four 2⅝ in. (6.7 cm) strips. Cross-cut these strips into eighteen 2⅝ in. (6.7 cm) squares and eighteen rectangles of each of these lengths:

4⅝ in. (11.7 cm)	5⅝ in. (14.3 cm)
7⅝ in. (19.4 cm)	9⅝ in. (24.5 cm)
10⅝ in. (27 cm)	

- Twenty-six 1⅝ in. (4.1 cm) strips. Cross-cut these strips into nineteen rectangles of each of these lengths:

4⅝ in. (11.7 cm)	5⅝ in. (14.3 cm)
7⅝ in. (19.4 cm)	8⅝ in. (21.9 cm)
10⅝ in. (27 cm)	11⅝ in. (29.6 cm)

- Four 6½ in. (16.5 cm) strips for border
- Six 3 in. (7.6 cm) strips for border

From each of the dark blue fabrics, cut:
- Three 2⅝ in. (6.7 cm) strips. Cross-cut these strips into two 2⅝ in. (6.7 cm) squares and two rectangles of each of these lengths:

4⅝ in. (11.7 cm)	5⅝ in. (14.3 cm)
7⅝ in. (19.4 cm)	9⅝ in. (24.5 cm)
10⅝ in. (27 cm)	

- Two 1⅝ in. (4.1 cm) strips. Cross-cut these strips into two rectangles of each of these lengths:

4⅝ in. (11.7 cm)	5⅝ in. (14.3 cm)
7⅝ in. (19.4 cm)	8⅝ in. (21.9 cm)
10⅝ in. (27 cm)	11⅝ in. (29.6 cm)

From each of the light blue fabrics, cut:
- Three 2⅝ in. (6.7 cm) strips. Cross-cut these strips into two 2⅝ in. (6.7 cm) squares and two rectangles of each of these lengths:

4⅝ in. (11.7 cm)	5⅝ in. (14.3 cm)
7⅝ in. (19.4 cm)	9⅝ in. (24.5 cm)
10⅝ in. (27 cm)	

- Two 1⅝ in. (4.1 cm) strips. Cross-cut these strips into two rectangles of each of these lengths:

4⅝ in. (11.7 cm)	5⅝ in. (14.3 cm)
7⅝ in. (19.4 cm)	8⅝ in. (21.9 cm)
10⅝ in. (27 cm)	11⅝ in. (29.6 cm)

From the extra light and dark blue fabric, cut:
- Sixteen 1½ in. (3.8 cm) strips

From the light blue fabric, cut:
- Eleven 3 in. (7.6 cm) strips for binding

making the quilt

sewing

Note Four different blocks make the design in this off-center Log Cabin quilt. Each diagram shows how to make blocks 1–4, but the written instructions are for a white/dark blue block 1. Blocks 2, 3, and 4 are constructed in the same way but the placement of each fabric is different. Follow the diagrams and the quilt photograph for fabric and color placement, noting where the strips of different widths are placed, as it is easy to get lost when sewing these blocks.

1. Sew a 2⅝ in. (6.7 cm) pink center square to the right-hand side of a 2⅝ in. (6.7 cm) white square and then press (see Diagram 1).

2. Sew a 4⅝ x 2⅝ in. (11.7 x 6.7 cm) white rectangle to the top of the unit and then press. Trim the unit to measure 4½ in. (11.4 cm) square (see Diagram 2).

3. Sew a 4⅝ x 2⅝ in. (11.7 x 6.7 cm) dark blue fabric rectangle to the right-hand side of the unit and then press (see Diagram 3).

4. Sew a 5⅝ x 1⅝ in. (14.3 x 4.1 cm) rectangle of the same dark blue fabric to the bottom of the unit and then press. Trim the unit to measure 5½ in. (14 cm) square (see Diagram 4).

5. Sew a 5⅝ x 2⅝ in. (14.3 x 6.7 cm) white rectangle to the left-hand side of the unit and then press. Trim the unit to measure 5½ x 7½ in. (14 x 19.1 cm) (see Diagram 5).

6. Sew a 7⅝ x 2⅝ in. (19.4 x 6.7 cm) white rectangle to the top of the unit and then press. Trim the unit to measure 7½ in. (19.1 cm) square (see Diagram 6).

7. Sew a 7⅝ x 1⅝ in. (19.4 x 4.1 cm) rectangle of the same dark blue fabric to the right-hand side of the unit and then press. Trim the unit to measure 7½ x 8½ in. (19.1 x 21.6 cm) (see Diagram 7).

8. Sew an 8⅝ x 2⅝ in. (21.9 x 6.7 cm) rectangle of the same dark blue fabric to the bottom of the unit and then press. Trim the unit to measure 8½ x 9½ in. (21.6 x 24.1 cm) (see Diagram 8).

9. Sew a 9⅝ x 2⅝ in. (24.5 x 6.7 cm) white rectangle to the left-hand side of the unit and then press. Trim the unit to measure 9½ x 10½ in. (24.1 x 26.7 cm) (see Diagram 9).

diagram 1

diagram 2

diagram 3

diagram 4

diagram 5

diagram 6

diagram 7

diagram 8

diagram 9

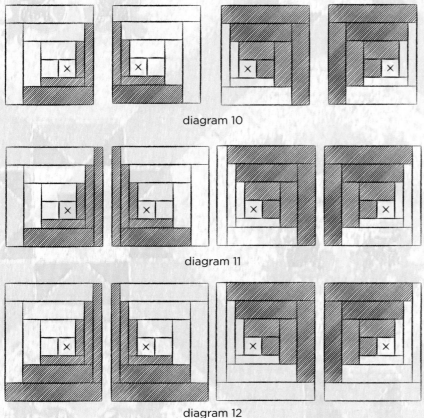

diagram 10

diagram 11

diagram 12

Tip There are a lot of different ways to sew a Log Cabin quilt. Although the blocks are deceptively simple, it's very easy to end up with a puckered block with a bump in the center if your piecing is not exact. To counteract this, I cut my strips wider and longer than I need to and trim after each round is added. This might seem like extra work but it will make all your Log Cabins straight, flat, and even at the end. All seams should be pressed away from the center of the block.

10. Sew a 10⅝ x 2⅝ in. (27 x 6.7 cm) white rectangle to the top of the unit and then press. Trim the unit to measure 10½ x 11½ in. (26.7 x 29.2 cm) (see Diagram 10).

11. Sew an 11⅝ x 1⅝ in. (29.6 x 4.1 cm) rectangle of the same dark blue fabric to the right-hand side of the unit and then press. Trim the unit to measure 11½ in. (29.2 cm) square (see Diagram 11).

12. Sew an 11⅝ x 2⅝ in. (29.6 x 6.7 cm) rectangle of the same dark blue fabric to the bottom of the unit and then press. Trim the unit to measure 11½ x 13½ in. (29.2 x 34.3 cm) (see Diagram 12).

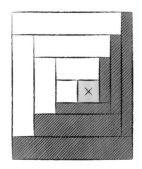 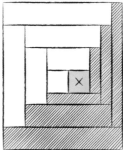 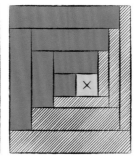

diagram 13

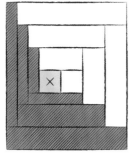 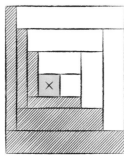 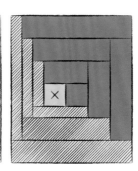

diagram 14

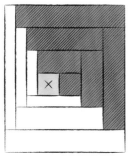 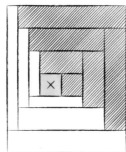 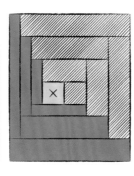

diagram 15

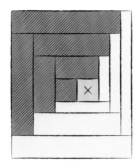 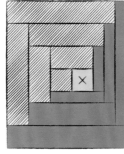 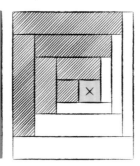

diagram 16

13. Make sixteen of each block: Block 1—one white/dark blue, eight white/light blue, seven dark blue/light blue (see Diagram 13) Block 2—one dark blue/white, eight light blue/white, seven light blue/dark blue (see Diagram 14) Block 3—one white/dark blue, eight white/light blue, seven dark blue/light blue (see Diagram 15)

Block 4—one dark blue/light blue, seven light blue/dark blue, eight light blue/white (see Diagram 16)

assembly

14. Referring to the quilt photograph, arrange the quilt blocks on your design wall or work surface (see Tip on page 126) in eight rows of eight blocks.

When you are satisfied with the arrangement, sew the blocks together into rows, and press the seams of each alternate row in opposite directions.

15. Sew the eight rows together and press the seams.

border

16. To make the letters for the words "Pitter Patter," cut pieces of fabric as needed, using light and dark blue 1½ in. (3.8 cm) strips for the letters and 3 in. (7.6 cm) white strips for the letters.

17. To make the letter P, cut a rectangle from the background fabric. You can use scissors, if preferred, as the shape doesn't have to be exact. Remember that the rectangle you are cutting will be the width of the top curve of the P and will determine the height of the letter. Sew a strip of blue along near the left-hand side of the rectangle for the upright of the P.

18. Sew a short blue strip along near the top of the rectangle, making sure it overlaps the previous strip. Sew second short piece coming down from this piece at an angle to start forming the curve of the P. Sew a third short piece to the bottom end of the previous piece to complete the curve. Finally sew a fourth piece horizontally to complete the letter.

19. Make the rest of the letters in the same manner. The letters are sewn the same way you would draw them. For example, with the letter R you would make the straight part first, and then the curved part on the right-hand side. Don't be afraid to add extra pieces of fabric to fill gaps or to make letters that look different from mine—that's the charm of this project.

20. Trim the letter blocks to 6½ in. (16.5 cm) wide. The block height doesn't matter as long as the edges of the blocks containing the letters are straight. You can trim the edges of the letters if necessary, as long as they still read clearly.

21. Measure the quilt top through the center from top to bottom to get the true measurement.

22. Remove the selvages from the remaining white 6½ in. (16.5 cm) strips. Sew the strips end-to-end to make one long strip. Depending on the size of your letters, you may not need them all.

23. Cut a 5½ x 6½ in. (14 x 16.5 cm) light blue rectangle. Arrange the letter blocks one above the other to spell "pitter" and then sew them to one long edge of the light blue rectangle. Sew a 6½ in. (16.5 cm) border strip to the other end of the letter strip. Press the seams. Trim the length of the pieced border strip to the measurement of your quilt top.

24. In the same way, sew and then trim a border strip using the letters to spell "patter."

25. Fold the two border strips in half and mark the centers with pins. Mark the sides of the quilt top in the same way. Matching pins, the ends, and with right sides together (and with the letters facing the correct way), pin and then sew the two border strips to the sides of the quilt top. Press the seams toward the borders.

backing, quilting, and binding

26. Cut the backing fabric crosswise into three 108 in. (274 cm) pieces. Remove the selvages and sew the

pieces together along the long edges to make the backing. Press the seams open and press the backing.

27. If you are going to do the quilting yourself, layer the backing, batting (wadding), and quilt top, following the instructions on page 131. If you are going to have the quilt professionally machine-quilted, do not layer it.

28. Quilt as desired. Mine was professionally machine-quilted with white thread in an all-over design with the words "pitter patter pitter patter" in cursive script.

29. Bind the quilt, following the instructions on page 133.

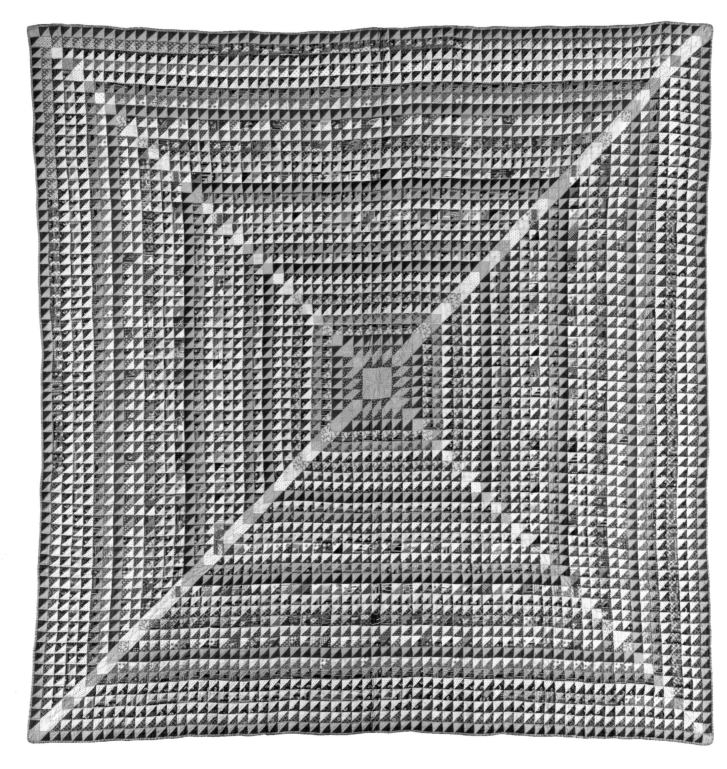

Triangles and Flying Geese Quilt
Artist unidentified
United States
1875–1900
Cotton
83 x 78"
Collection American Folk Art Museum, New York
Gift of Leo Rabkin, 2008.20.1
Photo by Gavin Ashworth

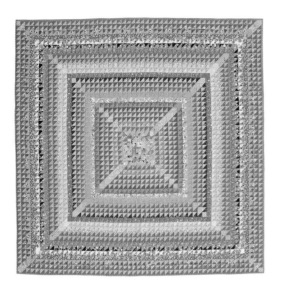

Mosaic
Sarah's direct interpretation

Triangles are among the most useful shapes in a quilter's arsenal. They can be combined and rearranged to form so many things—a star, an arrow, a pyramid, a square, a flag, a rectangle, or a pinwheel. They can also be used to direct movement in a quilt; if they all face in the same direction they can orient the visual impact of a border; if they face toward each other they can attract the eye to the center of a quilt. Triangles placed randomly all over a quilt can suggest chaos or tumult. If arranged sitting on their bases, triangles suggest solidity and structure, while if tipped at an angle or on their points the shapes can trick the eye.

I love to piece triangles, including 60-degree triangles and quarter-square triangles, but, most of all, the simplicity and versatility of the half-square triangle never fails to

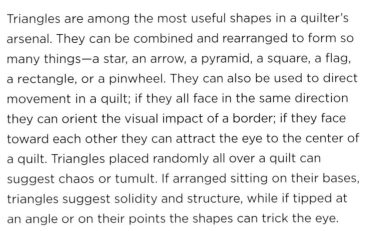

simple shapes

capture my imagination. The half-square triangle is the most basic of quilt piecing units, after squares and rectangles. There are many different ways to piece these shapes, but I always come back to the same tried and true methods when piecing triangles; as long as you are respectful of bias edges when piecing and pressing, triangles are simple and quick to sew together.

The two new quilts in this chapter both make use of triangles but in different ways from the antique quilt. The browns and creams of the original quilt are dynamic yet understated, while both Mosaic and Ebb and Flow shout color. All three are medallion quilts, built from the center out in concentric rounds. The rings of triangles all pointing in the same direction in Mosaic are full of energy, color, and life. Although the piecing in this quilt is repetitive and there are a lot of triangle units to make, the exercise in color balance, and the excitement that comes from watching the pattern develop as you add each round, are satisfying and result in a quilt that will always elicit a "wow" response.

The triangles in Ebb and Flow are essential to the design, but in a quieter way. The impact is made by the bars of color that form the quilt's central design, but the triangles in the corner create interest and movement.

Ebb and Flow
Sarah's modern reinterpretation

finished size

Double-bed size quilt or throw, 80 in. (208 cm) square

Note All strips are cut across the width of the fabric from fold to selvage, and seams are stitched with right sides together using a ¼ in. (6 mm) seam allowance unless otherwise stated.

Tip This quilt can easily be made larger by adding extra rounds. The strips for each round increase by two triangles each time. To make a queen-size (UK: king-size) quilt, you'll need another four rounds, and to make a king-size (UK: super-king-size) quilt, you'll need another ten rounds. Adjust the material requirements accordingly.

mosaic

I love this quilt but I will admit to feeling very glad to see the back of half-square triangles by the end! The result reminds me of tiled floors in Roman baths, although a lot brighter.

Each round of this quilt is comprised of a "triangle" fabric and a "background" fabric. The background fabric is lighter in color, and is on the inside edge of the row (facing toward the center of the quilt). The triangle fabric is darker in color and faces toward the outside edge of the quilt—i.e., the triangle is pointing to the center, with the flat edge facing out. This contrast will create the sharp rows of triangles needed to form the pattern. Rather than specify the fabric colors required for this quilt, the material requirements have been given as "triangle" and "background" fabrics.

material requirements

- Triangle fabrics (see project introduction):
  4 in. (10 cm) of the same fabric for rounds 1 and 2
  1¼ yd (1.2 m) of the same fabric for rounds 3, 11, 18, and 25
  6 in. (15 cm) each for rounds 4, 5, 6, and 7
  8 in. (20 cm) each for rounds 8, 9, and 10
  11 in. (28 cm) each for rounds 12, 13, 14, 15, and 16
  13 in. (31 cm) each for rounds 17, 19, and 20
  16 in. (40 cm) each for rounds 21, 22, 23, and 24

- Background fabrics (see project introduction):
  10 in. (25 cm) of the same fabric for rounds 1, 2, and center
  1¼ yd (1.2 m) of the same fabric for rounds 3, 11, 18, and 25
  6 in. (15 cm) each for rounds 4, 5, 6, and 7
  8 in. (20 cm) each for rounds 8, 9, and 10
  11 in. (28 cm) each for rounds 12, 13, 14, and 15
  13 in. (31 cm) each for rounds 16, 17, 19, and 20
  16 in. (40 cm) each for rounds 21, 22, and 23
  18 in. (45 cm) for round 24

- 28 in. (72 cm) pink-and-white striped fabric for the binding
- 5 yd (4.7 m) backing fabric
- 88 in. (228 cm) square cotton batting (wadding)
- Cotton thread for piecing
- Rotary cutter, mat, and ruler
- Sewing machine
- General sewing supplies

cutting

From the triangle and background fabrics, cut:

• 2⅜ in. (6 cm) strips. Cross-cut the strips into squares, and cross-cut these on one diagonal into half-square triangles (see page 126). The quantities of strips, squares, and triangles for each round are listed below. (Remember that rows 3, 11, 18, and 25 are all cut from the same fabrics.)

Quantities to cut from each of the triangle fabrics:

• Rounds 1 and 2—one strip, sixteen squares into thirty-two triangles
• Round 3—one strip, fourteen squares into twenty-eight triangles
• Round 4—two strips, eighteen squares into thirty-six triangles
• Round 5—two strips, twenty-two squares into forty-four triangles
• Round 6—two strips, twenty-six squares into fifty-two triangles
• Round 7—two strips, thirty squares into sixty triangles
• Round 8—three strips, thirty-four squares into sixty-eight triangles
• Round 9—three strips, thirty-eight squares into seventy-six triangles
• Round 10—three strips, forty-two squares into eighty-four triangles

• Round 11—three strips, forty-six squares into ninety-two triangles
• Round 12—four strips, fifty squares into one hundred triangles
• Round 13—four strips, fifty-four squares into 108 triangles
• Round 14—four strips, fifty-eight squares into 116 triangles
• Round 15—four strips, sixty-two squares into 124 triangles
• Round 16—four strips, sixty-six squares into 132 triangles
• Round 17—five strips, seventy squares into 140 triangles
• Round 18—five strips, seventy-four squares into 148 triangles
• Round 19—five strips, seventy-eight squares into 156 triangles
• Round 20—six strips, eighty-two squares into 164 triangles
• Round 21—six strips, eighty-six squares into 172 triangles
• Round 22—six strips, ninety squares into 180 triangles
• Round 23—six strips, ninety-four squares into 188 triangles
• Round 24—six strips, ninety-eight squares into 196 triangles
• Round 25—seven strips, 102 squares into 204 triangles

Tip Cut the triangles first, and then trim the remaining strip to 2 in. (5.1 cm) to cut the 2 in. (5.1 cm) squares.

Quantities to cut from each of the background fabrics:

• Rounds 1 and 2—two strips, sixteen squares into thirty-two triangles, and eight 2 in. (5.1 cm) squares. Also cut one 5 in. (12.9 cm) square from this fabric for the quilt center.
• Round 3—two strips, fourteen squares into twenty-eight triangles, and four 2 in. (5.1 cm) squares
• Round 4—two strips, eighteen squares into thirty-six triangles, and four 2 in. (5.1 cm) squares
• Round 5—two strips, twenty-two squares into forty-four triangles, and four 2 in. (5.1 cm) squares
• Round 6—two strips, twenty-six squares into fifty-two triangles, and four 2 in. (5.1 cm) squares
• Round 7—two strips, thirty squares into sixty triangles, and four 2 in. (5.1 cm) squares

• Round 8—three strips, thirty-four squares into sixty-eight triangles, and four 2 in. (5.1 cm) squares
• Round 9—three strips, thirty-eight squares into seventy-six triangles, and four 2 in. (5.1 cm) squares
• Round 10—three strips, forty-two squares into eighty-four triangles, and four 2 in. (5.1 cm) squares
• Round 11—three strips, forty-six squares into ninety-two triangles, and four 2 in. (5.1 cm) squares
• Round 12—four strips, fifty squares into one hundred triangles, and four 2 in. (5.1 cm) squares
• Round 13—four strips, fifty-four squares into 108 triangles, and four 2 in. (5.1 cm) squares
• Round 14—four strips, fifty-eight squares into 116 triangles, and four 2 in. (5.1 cm) squares
• Round 15—four strips, sixty-two squares into 124 triangles, and four 2 in. (5.1 cm) squares
• Round 16—five strips, sixty-six squares into 132 triangles, and four 2 in. (5.1 cm) squares
• Round 17—five strips, seventy squares into 140 triangles, and four 2 in. (5.1 cm) squares
• Round 18—five strips, seventy-four squares into 148 triangles, and four 2 in. (5.1 cm) squares
• Round 19—five strips, seventy-eight squares into 156 triangles, and four 2 in. (5.1 cm) squares
• Round 20—six strips, eighty-two squares into 164 triangles, and four 2 in. (5.1 cm) squares
• Round 21—six strips, eighty-six squares into 172 triangles, and four 2 in. (5.1 cm) squares
• Round 22—six strips, ninety squares into 180 triangles, and four 2 in. (5.1 cm) squares
• Round 23—six strips, ninety-four squares into 188 triangles, and four 2 in. (5.1 cm) squares
• Round 24—seven strips, ninety-eight squares into 196 triangles, and four 2 in. (5.1 cm) squares
• Round 25—seven strips, 102 squares into 204 triangles, and four 2 in. (5.1 cm) squares

From the pink-and-white striped fabric, cut:

• Nine 3 in. (7.6 cm) strips for binding

making the quilt
sewing and assembly

diagram 1

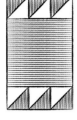

diagram 2   diagram 3

1. Referring to the quilt photograph, arrange the pieces on your design wall or work surface (see Tip on page 126), to help you balance the color.

Round 1
2. Sew twelve round 1 triangles and backgrounds in pairs along the diagonal edges; each unit should be 2 in. (5.1 cm) square. Press the seams toward the dark fabric and trim the "ears" (see Diagram 1).

Tip Trimming the "ears" is very important in this quilt—it reduces bulk and helps keep the points of the triangles accurate.

3. Sew the units into four strips of three, ensuring that all the triangles are facing the correct direction—i.e., facing one way in two strips and facing the other way in two strips (see Diagram 2). Press the seams in the same direction.

4. Pin and then sew two of the same triangle sets to the top and bottom of the 5 in. (12.9 cm) center square, with the fabric that is different from the center square facing inward (see Diagram 3). Press the seams toward the center.

5. Sew a 2 in. (5.1 cm) center-fabric square to each end of the remaining two strips. Pin and then sew a strip to each side of the center square (see Diagram 4). Press the seams toward the center.

Round 2
6. Make four more strips using the same combination of fabrics, this time with five sets of triangles in each strip. Ensure that the triangles are pointing in the correct direction as before.

7. Sew two of the same triangle sets to the top and bottom of the quilt top, with center fabric facing inward this time, so that they touch the previous round's center-fabric triangles (see Diagram 5). Press the seams toward the center.

8. Sew a 2 in. (5.1 cm) center-fabric square to each end of the remaining two strips. Sew a strip to each side of the quilt top in the same way (see Diagram 6). This is the only time in the quilt that the position of the triangle fabric and the background fabric is reversed. Press the seams toward the center.

Round 3
9. Sew twenty-eight round 3 triangles and backgrounds in pairs along the diagonal edges as before. Sew the units into four strips of seven, ensuring the triangles are facing the correct direction. Press the seams in the same direction.

10. Pin and then sew two of the same triangle sets to the top and bottom of the quilt top, with the long edge of the background-fabric triangle facing toward the center. Press the seams toward the center.

11. Sew a 2 in. (5.1 cm) background-fabric square to each end of the remaining two strips. Pin and then sew a strip to each side of the quilt top (see Diagram 7). Press the seams toward the center.

Rounds 4–25
12. Continue to sew sets of triangles into pairs and then into strips, one round at a time. Pin and then sew each round to the quilt top, as before. The pattern repeats itself in the same manner in each round, with two extra triangles in the strips for each round.

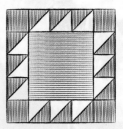

diagram 4

diagram 5

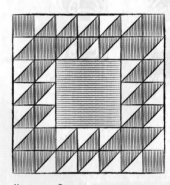

diagram 6

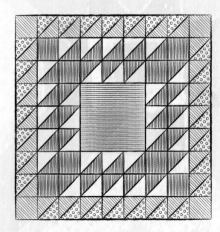

diagram 7

backing, quilting, and binding

13. Cut the backing fabric crosswise into two 90 in. (235 cm) lengths. Remove the selvages (selvedges) and sew the pieces together along the middle seam to make the backing. Press the seam allowances open and press the backing.

14. If you are going to do the quilting yourself, layer the backing, batting (wadding), and quilt top, following the instructions on page 131. If you are going to have the quilt professionally machine-quilted, do not layer it.

15. Quilt as desired. Mine was professionally machine-quilted in an all-over pattern.

16. Bind the quilt, following the instructions on page 133.

ebb and flow

This quilt is so calm and peaceful. To me, it feels like an island surrounded by a cool blue and green sea. Not only is the combination of warm colors surrounded by cool ones serenely appealing, but a lovely focus is created toward the center of the quilt while, at the same time, your eye is drawn away by the black-and-white triangles. Ebb and Flow would look fantastic made in a rainbow gradation of colors, or even with bright, colorful triangles radiating out over a low-volume background of strips.

finished size

Queen-size (UK: king-size) bed quilt, 96½ in. (246 cm) square

Note All strips are cut across the width of the fabric from fold to selvage, and seams are stitched with right sides together using a ¼ in. (6 mm) seam allowance unless otherwise stated.

Note All solid fabrics used are Rowan Shot Cottons.

material requirements

- One 8½ in. (21.6 cm) square ice fabric for center
- 6 in. (15 cm) each of quartz and pudding fabrics for rounds 1 and 2
- 8 in. (20 cm) each of lilac and pink fabrics for rounds 3 and 4
- 12 in. (30 cm) each of apricot, tangerine, and sunshine fabrics for rounds 5, 6, and 7
- 14 in. (35 cm) each of pumpkin and nut fabrics for rounds 8 and 9
- 16 in. (40 cm) each of sandstone, artemisia, and dill fabrics for rounds 10, 11, and 12
- 18 in. (46 cm) each of sprout, honeydew, and viridian fabrics for rounds 13, 14, and 15
- 22 in. (56 cm) of apple fabric for round 16

- 24 in. (61 cm) each of squash, cactus, jade, and sky fabrics for rounds 17, 18, 19, and 20
- 26 in. (66 cm) each of aqua and violet fabrics for rounds 21 and 22
- 30 in. (76 cm) black-and-white print fabric for triangles and squares
- 1 yd (1 m) black-and-white fabric for binding
- 8½ yd (7.8 m) backing fabric
- 102 in. (260 cm) square cotton batting (wadding)
- Cotton thread for piecing
- Rotary cutter, mat, and ruler
- Sewing machine
- General sewing supplies

cutting

From all the colored fabrics (i.e., not black-and-white), cut:

- One 2⅞ in. (7.3 cm) strip from each fabric. Cross-cut each strip into four squares, and cross-cut these on one diagonal into eight half-square triangles. For the even-numbered rows only, trim the remaining part of each strip to 2½ in. (6.3 cm) and cross-cut into four 2½ in. (6.3 cm) squares.

From the quartz and pudding fabrics, cut:

- One 2½ in. (6.3 cm) strip from each fabric

From the lilac and pink fabrics, cut:

- Two 2½ in. (6.3 cm) strips from each fabric

From the apricot, tangerine, and sunshine fabrics, cut:

- Three 2½ in. (6.3 cm) strips from each fabric

From the pumpkin and nut fabrics, cut:

- Four 2½ in. (6.3 cm) strips from each fabric

From the sandstone, artemisia, and dill fabrics, cut:

- Five 2½ in. (6.3 cm) strips from each fabric

From the sprout, honeydew, and viridian fabrics, cut:

- Six 2½ in. (6.3 cm) strips from each fabric

From the apple fabric, cut:

- Seven 21½ in. (6.3 cm) strips from each fabric

From the squash, cactus, jade, and sky fabrics, cut:

- Eight 2½ in. (6.3 cm) strips from each fabric

From the aqua and violet fabrics, cut:

- Nine 2½ in. (6.3 cm) strips from each fabric

From the black-and-white print fabric, cut:

- Three 2½ in. (6.3 cm) strips. Cross-cut the strips into forty-four squares, which will be the corners for all the odd-numbered rows.
- Seven 2⅞ in. (7.3 cm) strips. Cross-cut the strips into eighty-eight squares. Cross-cut the squares on one diagonal into 176 half-square triangles.

From the black-and-white fabric, cut:

- Eleven 3 in. (7.6 cm) strips for binding

making the quilt
sewing and assembly

Before you begin piecing, be sure to read this! The quilt is constructed in rounds, working from the center outward. Although construction is not difficult, it is very easy to end up with a three-dimensional quilt if you aren't careful. If you don't measure, cut, and pin every row carefully, the quilt will not grow in flat rounds. Instead, it will have a bump in the center and refuse to lie flat. Take the extra time to follow the directions and your quilt will be flat.

diagram 1

diagram 2

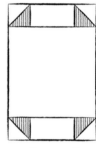

diagram 3

Round 1

1. Sew eight quartz triangles and eight black-and-white triangles in pairs along the diagonal edges. Each unit should be 2½ in. (6.3 cm) square. Press the seams toward the black-and-white fabric and trim the "ears" (see Diagram 1).

2. From the 2½ in. (6.3 cm) strip of quartz fabric, cut four 2½ x 4½ in. (6.3 x 11.4 cm) rectangles. Sew a triangle unit to each end of each rectangle, with the diagonal sloping toward the end of the strip (see Diagram 2)—this is the orientation for an odd-numbered round.

3. Pin and then sew one of these pieced strips to the top and a second one to the bottom of the ice center square (see Diagram 3). Press the seams toward the center square.

Tip It is important to pin-mark the center of the strip and the center of the square. Match the pin marks and then pin the ends. Pin in between and ease the pieces, if required, before stitching. Repeat this with every strip before you sew it to the quilt.

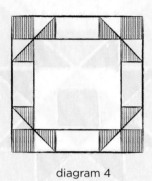
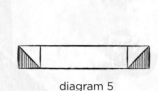
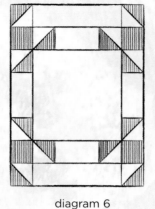
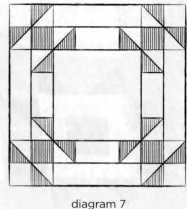

diagram 4   diagram 5   diagram 6   diagram 7

4. Sew a black-and-white 2½ in. (6.3 cm) square to each end of the remaining two quartz strips. Sew one of these pieced strips to each side of the center square in the same manner, taking care to pin, check the orientation of the triangles, and match the seams (see Diagram 4). Press the seams toward the center square.

Round 2

5. Sew eight pudding triangles and eight black-and-white triangles in pairs along the diagonal edges. Press the seams toward the black-and-white fabric and trim the "ears."

6. From the 2½ in. (6.3 cm) strip of pudding fabric, cut four 2½ x 8½ in. (6.3 x 21.6 cm) rectangles. Sew a triangle unit to each end of each rectangle, with the diagonal sloping toward the center of the strip (see Diagram 5)—this is the orientation for an even-numbered round.

7. Pin and then sew one of these pieced strips to the top and a second one to the bottom of the quilt top (see Diagram 6). Press the seams toward the center square.

8. This is an even-numbered round, so sew a 2½ in. (6.3 cm) pudding-fabric square—*not* a black-and-white square—to each end of the remaining two pudding strips. Pin and then sew one of these pieced strips to each side of the quilt top (see Diagram 7). Press the seams toward the center square.

Rounds 3–22

9. Continue to cut, pin, sew, and then press each round in this manner, repeating the patterns for odd- and even-numbered rounds. The length of the cut strips for each side increases by 4 in. (10.2 cm) each time; so round 3 will be 12½ in. (31.8 cm), round 4 will be 16½ in. (42 cm), and so on.

10. From round 3 onward, join all the strips that are cut for that round into one long strip, and then cut the required lengths from this long strip. Do not be tempted just to sew the strip on and then cut it off to the right length, because this will lead to a puckered block that will not lie flat. Joining the strips also ensures that all the joins are in different places on the quilt, so that your eye isn't drawn to the same place on every round. Continue measuring, pinning, stitching, and pressing until the twenty-two rounds are attached.

backing, quilting, and binding

11. Cut the backing fabric crosswise into three 102 in. (259 cm) lengths. Remove the selvages and sew the pieces together along the long edges to make the backing. Press the seam allowances open and press the backing.

12. If you are going to do the quilting yourself, layer the backing, batting (wadding), and quilt top, following the instructions on page 131. If you are going to have the quilt professionally machine-quilted, do not layer it.

13. Quilt as desired. Mine was professionally machine-quilted in an all-over design.

14. Bind the quilt, following the instructions on page 133.

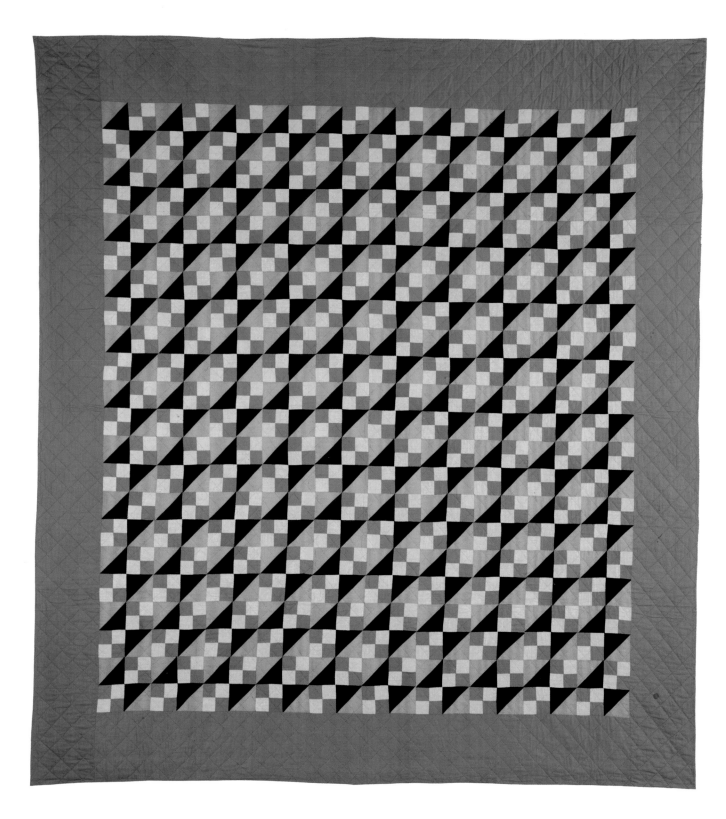

Four-Patch and Triangles Quilt
Barbara Zook Peachey (1848–1930)
Pennsylvania
1910–1920
Cotton
85½ x 78¾"
Collection American Folk Art Museum, New York
Gift of Mr. and Mrs. William B. Wigton, 1984.25.12
Photo by Schecter Lee

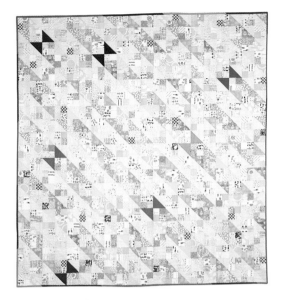

Keep It Down!
Sarah's direct interpretation

For many people, when they think of quilts the first image that comes to mind will be something like the Amish quilt, opposite. The distinctive Amish style, with its meticulous, exacting workmanship and striking use of solids, has become synonymous with American quilting. But quilting was not brought to the Americas by the Amish, as is often assumed. In fact, Amish women learned to quilt from their "English" neighbors, as they refer to anyone non-Amish.

The Amish are descended from Swiss-German Anabaptists who emigrated to America in large numbers

amish traditions

Ink Pink
Sarah's modern reinterpretation

in the early eighteenth century. Adornment and art for its own sake are frowned upon by the Amish, but the beauty of their quilts is a by-product of their form and function.

Amish patterns are beautiful in their simplicity, featuring graphic patterns in solid fabrics. Many quilts incorporate black, which enables the other jewel-like colors to sparkle. Appliqué is considered too frivolous and is generally not used, nor are printed fabrics.

Amish hand-quilting is known the world over for its intricacy. Many quilts were pieced on a treadle sewing machine, but the quilting was always worked by hand. Living as a community is part of the Amish way of life and so the quilts are often hand-quilted on a large frame by a group of women working in a "bee."

Amish quilters are still active in the quilting community, operating quilt shops and selling their quilts, as well as sewing for their families. Amish quilting has become a huge source of inspiration for modern quilters and those who enjoy working with the wide rainbow of solids that are currently available.

keep it down!

Here's a perfect example of how you can use a traditional layout but change the colors and the value to create a whole new interpretation. This quilt is the same layout as the original but features low-contrast fabrics plus a smattering of jewel-toned solids.

I used a wider variety of fabrics than are listed here—I love to have as many different fabrics in a quilt as I can! While it's not practical to give all of them as material requirements in a book, it doesn't mean you can't slip a few extras or random squares from your scrap bin into the mix to spice things up.

Choosing the fabric to make a low-volume quilt like this can be tricky. Make sure you have fabrics with plenty of different prints and scales of pattern, but keep them predominately white. The grays that make the diagonal strips need to be quiet, too, but with a more solid gray background and not a lot of white. You may need to search for the right fabrics but many shops have a black-and-white or low-contrast fabric section, so hunt them out. Of course, you could choose some wonderful solids and make the quilt just like the antique one so that everything old is new again.

finished size

Large throw, or quilt for end of a double bed, 80½ in. (205.2 cm) wide x 84½ in. (215.4 cm) long

Note This quilt can easily be made larger or smaller by changing the number of blocks and rows. To make a single-bed size quilt, 57 x 94 in. (145 x 239 cm), make twenty-four rows of fourteen blocks. To make a queen-bed size (UK: king-size) quilt, 94 in. (239 cm) square, make twenty-four rows of twenty-four blocks. To make a king-bed size (UK: superking-size) quilt, 102 in. (259 cm) square, make twenty-six rows of twenty-six blocks.

Note All strips are cut across the width of the fabric from fold to selvage, and seams are stitched with right sides together using a ¼ in. (6 mm) seam allowance unless otherwise stated.

material requirements

- 2 yd (1.8 m) main white print for half-square triangles
- 10 in. (25 cm) each of seven assorted gray fabrics
- 8 in. (20 cm) each of seven jewel-toned solids (green, dark blue, medium blue, yellow, orange, light green, and purple)
- 14 in. (15 cm) each of ten assorted predominately white fabrics
- 5 yd (4.6 m) backing fabric
- 86 x 90 in. (219 x 230 cm) piece cotton batting (wadding)
- Cotton thread for piecing
- Rotary cutter, mat, and ruler
- Sewing machine
- General sewing supplies

cutting

From the main white print fabric, cut:
- Fourteen 4⅞ in. (12.4 cm) strips. Cross-cut the strips into 105 squares. Cross-cut the squares on one diagonal into 210 half-square triangles.

From the seven assorted gray fabrics, cut:
- Two 4⅞ in. (12.4 cm) strips from each fabric. Cross-cut the strips into ninety-eight squares. Cross-cut the squares on one diagonal into 196 half-square triangles.

From the seven jewel-toned fabrics, cut:
- One 4⅞ in. (12.4 cm) square from each fabric. Cross-cut the squares on one diagonal into fourteen half-square triangles.
- Cut the remaining fabric into seven 3 in. (7.6 cm) strips for binding.

From the ten assorted predominately white fabrics, cut:
- Five 2½ in. (6.3 cm) strips from each fabric. Cross-cut the strips into 840 squares (see Tip).

Tip I like to cut each fabric into a square and sew the separate squares together, instead of using quicker piecing methods. This is my own personal preference and results in a scrappier, more mixed finish. If you prefer to use the quick piecing method to make the Four Patches, do not cut the strips into squares but leave them in 2½ in. (6.3 cm) strips and start at step 2.

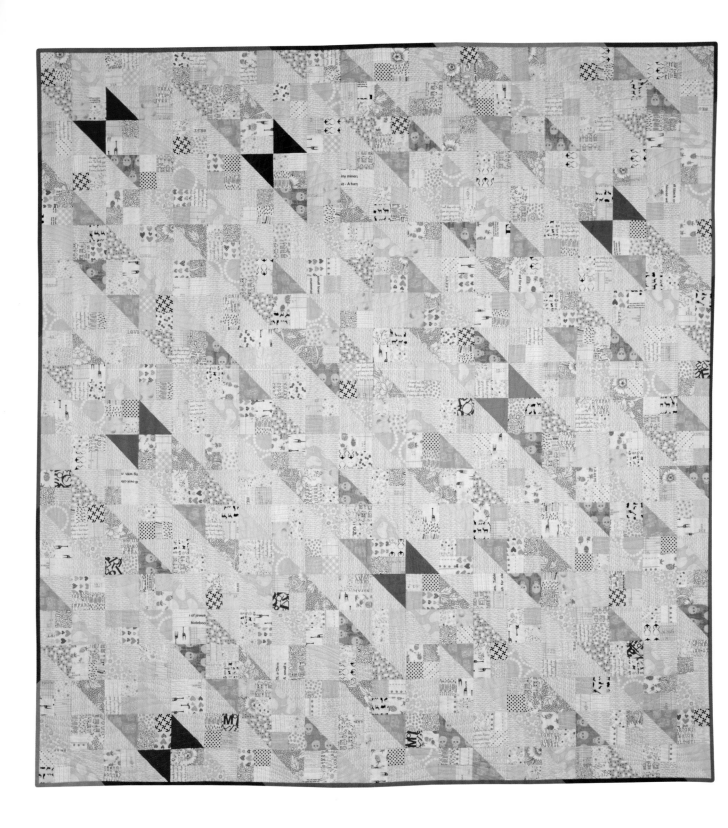

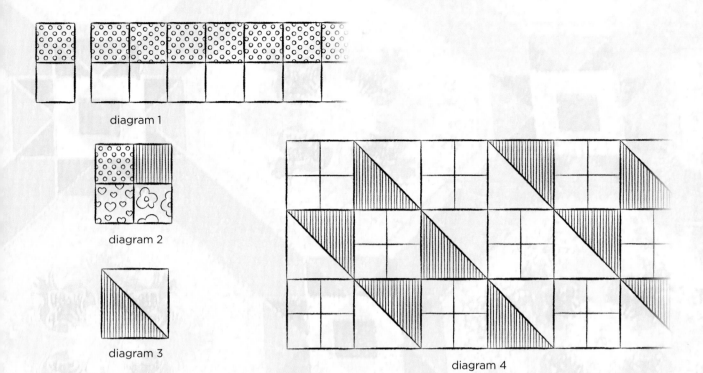

diagram 1

diagram 2

diagram 3

diagram 4

making the quilt

sewing

1. If you are using 2½ in. (6.3 cm) squares, as I did (see Tip), mix all the squares and choose random pairs from the pile. Don't worry about what goes with what, just make sure you don't have two of the same together. Sew the squares into 420 pairs and omit step 2.

2. If you prefer to use the quick piecing method instead, omit step 1 and sew the strips together into pairs along the long edges. Press the seam to one side and then cut the strip into 2½ x 4½ in. (6.3 x 11.4 cm) units (see Diagram 1)—you need 420. Ensure you keep the pieces square to the top and bottom of the strip to prevent making uneven cuts. If the strips get out of alignment, square the edge of the fabric up again before you continue cutting.

3. Sew two sets of pairs together to make a Four Patch block, which is 4½ in. (11.4 cm) square (see Diagram 2). Make 210 of these blocks.

4. Sew the white print triangles and gray triangles in pairs along the diagonal edges. Sew the remaining fourteen white print triangles to the fourteen jewel-toned triangles in the same way. Press all the seams to one side and trim off the "ears." Make 210 of these blocks (see Diagram 3).

assembly

5. Referring to the quilt photograph, arrange the quilt blocks on your design wall or work surface (see Tip on page 126) so that they are in twenty-one rows of twenty blocks, with the triangles forming diagonal lines across the quilt from top left to bottom right (see Diagram 4). Ensure that you turn the triangles in the correct direction to make the pattern.

6. The seven pairs of jewel-toned blocks in my quilt are in these positions:

Green	Row 2, block 3
	Row 3, block 2
Dark blue	Row 3, block 8
	Row 4, block 7
Medium blue	Row 5, block 18
	Row 6, block 17
Yellow	Row 10, block 15
	Row 11, block 14
Orange	Row 11, block 4
	Row 12, block 3
Light green	Row 15, block 12
	Row 16, block 11
Purple	Row 20, block 5
	Row 21, block 4

If you prefer, include more or fewer colored triangles or change the positioning.

7. When you are pleased with the arrangement, sew the blocks into twenty-one rows of twenty blocks, pressing the seams of adjacent rows in opposite directions. Sew the twenty-one rows together and press the seams to one side, in the same direction.

backing, quilting, and binding

8. Cut the backing fabric into two 90 in. (230 cm) pieces. Remove the selvages and sew the pieces together along the long edges to make the backing. Press the seam open and press the backing.

9. If you are going to do the quilting yourself, layer the backing, batting (wadding), and quilt top, following the instructions on page 131. If you are going to have the quilt professionally machine-quilted, do not layer it.

10. Quilt as desired. Mine was professionally machine-quilted in an all-over curvy design.

11. Bind the quilt, following the instructions on page 133.

ink pink

This modern Four Patch design takes all the elements of the antique quilt and mixes them up like a salad. The half-square triangles and squares are still there, as is the diagonal layout. Instead of orderly lines, though, the squares are used as negative space between different-sized triangles for a jumbled effect. This quilt would look fantastic in black, white, and yellow, too.

material requirements

- 32 in. (81.5 cm) natural linen for half-square triangles
- 32 in. (81.5 cm) hot pink print for half-square triangles
- 12 in. (30.5 cm) each of eight assorted pink print fabrics for squares
- 12 in. (30.5 cm) aqua print fabric for inner border
- 30 in. (76 cm) orange print fabric for outer border
- 26 in. (66 cm) striped fabric for binding
- 4½ yd. (4.1 m) backing fabric
- 78 in. (2 m) square piece cotton batting (wadding)
- Cotton thread for piecing
- Rotary cutter, mat, and ruler
- Sewing machine
- General sewing supplies

finished size

Large throw, 68½ in. (174.6 cm) square

Note All strips are cut across the width of the fabric from fold to selvage, and seams are stitched with right sides together using a ¼ in. (6 mm) seam allowance unless otherwise stated.

cutting

From the natural linen fabric, cut:
- Two 2⅞ in. (7.3 cm) strips. Cross-cut the strips into sixteen squares. Cross-cut the squares on one diagonal into thirty-one half-square triangles. (There will be one spare triangle.)
- Two 4⅞ in. (12.4 cm) strips. Cross-cut the strips into twelve squares. Cross-cut the squares on one diagonal into twenty-three half-square triangles. (There will be one spare triangle.)
- One 6⅞ in. (17.5 cm) strip. Cross-cut the strip into six squares. Cross-cut the squares on one diagonal into twelve half-square triangles.
- One 8⅞ in. (22.6 cm) strip. Cross-cut the strip into four squares. Cross-cut the squares on one diagonal into eight half-square triangles.

From the hot pink print fabric, cut:
- Two 2⅞ in. (7.3 cm) strips. Cross-cut the strips into sixteen squares. Cross-cut the squares on one diagonal into thirty-one half-square triangles. (There will be one spare triangle.)
- Two 4⅞ in. (12.4 cm) strips. Cross-cut the strips into twelve squares. Cross-cut the squares on one diagonal into twenty-three half-square triangles. (There will be one spare triangle.)
- One 6⅞ in. (17.5 cm) strip. Cross cut the strip into six squares. Cross cut the squares on one diagonal into twelve half-square triangles.
- One 8⅞ in. (22.6 cm) strip. Cross-cut the strip into four squares. Cross-cut the squares on one diagonal into eight half-square triangles.

From the eight assorted pink print fabrics, cut:
- Four 2½ in. (6.3 cm) strips from each fabric. Cross-cut the strips into 542 squares.

From the aqua print fabric, cut:
- Seven 1½ in. (3.7 cm) strips for inner border

From the orange print fabric, cut:
- Eight 3½ in. (8.9 cm) strips for outer border

From the striped fabric cut:
- Eight 3 in. (7.6 cm) strips for binding

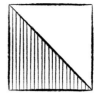

diagram 1

making the quilt

sewing

1. Sew the natural triangles and hot pink triangles in pairs along the diagonal edge, pairing the triangles of the same size. Press the seams to one side and trim off the "ears" (see Diagram 1).

assembly

2. Referring to the quilt photograph on page 107, arrange the half-square triangle units on your design wall or work surface (see Tip on page 126), to form diagonal lines across the quilt top from top left to bottom right, and then arrange the pink squares after that. Ensure that you turn the triangles in the correct direction to make the pattern.

3. When you are pleased with the color arrangement, start with the portion shown on the left of Diagram 2 and join the pieces to form the thirteen little units indicated by the numbers, and then join these units into one long panel. Follow this basic process to assemble the other nine panels shown in this diagram, paying close attention to how many squares and triangle units are in each panel. Where there are red dots on a square in the diagram, leave the seam open by 1 in. (2.5 cm) from the jagged edge—these partial seams will be completed later.

4. Now sew the pieced panels together, as shown in Diagram 3—the arrows and red lines in the diagram show where the panels are joined. Where there are red dots on a square, leave the seam open by 1 in. (2.5 cm) as in step 3.

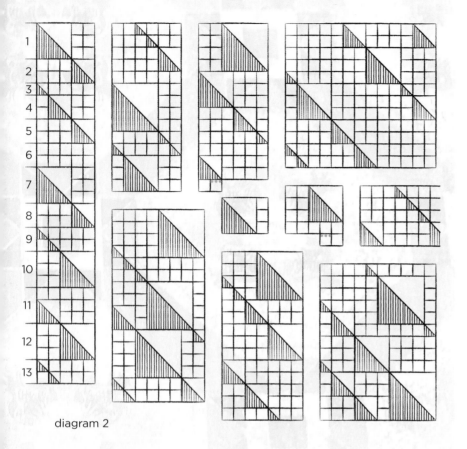

diagram 2

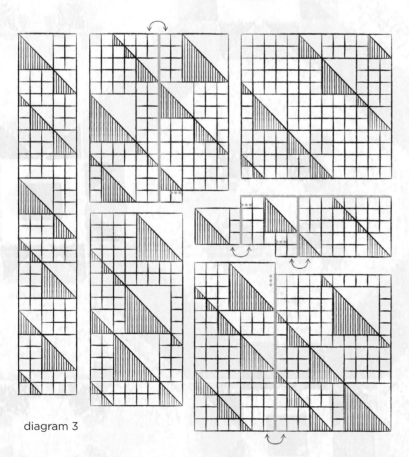

diagram 3

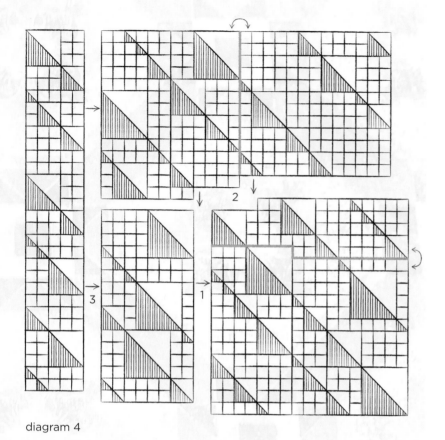

diagram 4

5. Sew the remaining sections together (see Diagram 4). Where there is a T-shaped seam, sew the longer edge together first, and then close the seam previously left open. The bottom section of the quilt is joined together first, then the top section and finally the long panel down the left-hand side, as indicated by the numbers and arrows in the diagram. Press. The completely joined panels are shown in Diagram 5, with the seams shown in red.

inner border

6. Sew the aqua print strips end-to-end to make one long strip. Measure your quilt top through the center from side to side—it should be 60½ in. (154.2 cm). If it is not, make a note of the measurement. From the long strip, cut two pieces to this measurement.

7. Fold the two border strips in half and mark the centers with pins. Mark the top and bottom of the quilt top in the same way. Matching the pins, the ends, and with right sides together, pin and then sew the inner border strips to the top and bottom of the quilt top. Press the seams toward the border.

8. Measure your quilt top through the center from top to bottom—it should be 62½ in. (159.2 cm). If it is not, make a note of the measurement. From the remaining long strip, cut two pieces to this measurement.

9. Fold the two border strips in half and mark the centers with pins. Mark the sides of the quilt top using the same method. In the same way as in step 7, pin and then sew the strips to the side edges of the quilt top. Press the seams toward the border.

outer border

10. Sew the orange print strips end-to-end to make one long strip. Measure your quilt top through the center from side to side—it should be 62½ in. (159.2 cm). If it is not, make a

diagram 5

note of the measurement. From the long strip, cut two pieces to this measurement. Attach these to the top and bottom edges as for the inner border, step 7. Press the seams toward the inner border.

11. Measure your quilt top through the center from side to side—it should be 68½ in. (174.6 cm). If it is not, make a note of the measurement. From the remaining long strip, cut two pieces to this measurement. Attach these to the

sides as for the inner border, step 9. Press the seams toward the inner border.

finishing

12. Cut the backing fabric into two 80 in. (204 cm) pieces. Remove the selvages and sew the pieces together along the long edges to make the backing. Press the seam open and press the backing.

13. If you are going to do the quilting yourself, layer the backing, batting (wadding), and quilt top, following the instructions on page 000. If you are going to have the quilt professionally machine-quilted, do not layer it.

14. Quilt as desired. Mine was professionally machine-quilted in an all-over curvy pattern.

15. Bind the quilt, following the instructions on page 133.

Pinwheel Sunflower Quilt
Mary Etta (Mrs. Edward Emmet) Bach (1872–1974)
Philadelphia
1930–1950
Cotton
97½ x 77"
Collection American Folk Art Museum, New York
Bequest of the estate of Mildred P. Bach, 1992.27.5
Photo by Gavin Ashworth

Planting
Sarah's direct interpretation

Quilting, like all crafts, comes and goes. There are notable periods when the craft explodes and becomes popular again after being out of fashion—we are living through one of these periods now!

The quilting resurgence that occurred in the United States between 1920 and 1950 was sparked at first by patterns designed to target women who wanted their homes to look bright, cheerful, and modern after the austerity of World War I. Post-war, new, cheerful, conversational prints in shades of green, yellow, pink, blue, peach, and lavender became available—these same shades are still reproduced today for 1930s conversational-print fabrics, and are loved by many quilters. The combination of these new fabrics, and a group of talented women

revival

Pretty Pinwheel
Sarah's modern reinterpretation

designing patterns specifically for this market, caused quilting's popularity to grow in leaps and bounds.

As the 1920s gave way to the Great Depression in the 1930s, a need to be thrifty, as well as a desire to socialize with other people and feel part of a community, gave quilting an even bigger boost. Scraps were swapped and bees were held, while newspapers and sales catalogs often published free quilt blocks and pattern pieces, along with advertisements for the fabric needed for the project.

Quilt kits were born during this time. Offered in newspapers, available by mail order, or sold through milliners' shops, the kits would provide the pattern and all the fabric needed to make a project. Some of the quilts in museum collections today are made from these popular kits. If you want to make the Planting quilt in the same fabrics as the original quilt, you shouldn't have any trouble finding 1930s reproduction fabrics at your local quilt store.

planting

The original 1930s quilt has had a revival here, with the clean lines of modern text and architectural print fabrics. Although I kept the scalloped border, I think its slightly different shape has stayed true to the more modern lines of the fabric.

Planting is charming enough to be made in reproduction fabrics, yet sharp enough for a modern nursery. Alternatively, make more clusters of flowers for a quilt for a larger bed. Four blocks across and down will make a queen- or king-size (UK: king- or superking-size) quilt, with a little border adjustment.

finished size

Crib (cot) size quilt, 54¼ in. (137.8 cm) wide x 69¼ in. (175.9 cm) long

Note All strips are cut across the width of the fabric from fold to selvage, and seams are stitched with right sides together using a ¼ in. (6 mm) seam allowance unless otherwise stated.

material requirements

- One fat eighth of eight different colored fabrics for pinwheels, or scrap fabrics totaling 24 in. (61 cm)
- 1¼ yd (1.2 m) green polka-dot fabric for leaves
- 2¼ yd (2.1 m) black-on-white patterned fabric for pinwheel background
- 4 in. (10.2 cm) black-and-white polka-dot fabric for center circles
- 2 yd (1.9 m) black-on-white patterned fabric for sashing and border
- 14 in. (35.6 cm) black-and-white patterned fabric for cornerstones
- 1¼ yd (1.2 m) black-and-white polka-dot fabric for binding
- 3½ yd (3.2 m) backing fabric
- 63 x 77 in. (160 x 196 cm) piece cotton batting (wadding)
- Piece of thin cardboard (a cereal box is ideal)

- Aluminum foil
- Straw needles
- Appliqué glue
- One sheet of template plastic (see page 137 for templates)
- Scissors for cutting template plastic
- Scissors for fabric and cardboard
- Black cotton thread for appliqué
- Cotton thread for piecing
- Rotary cutter, mat and ruler
- Sewing machine
- General sewing supplies

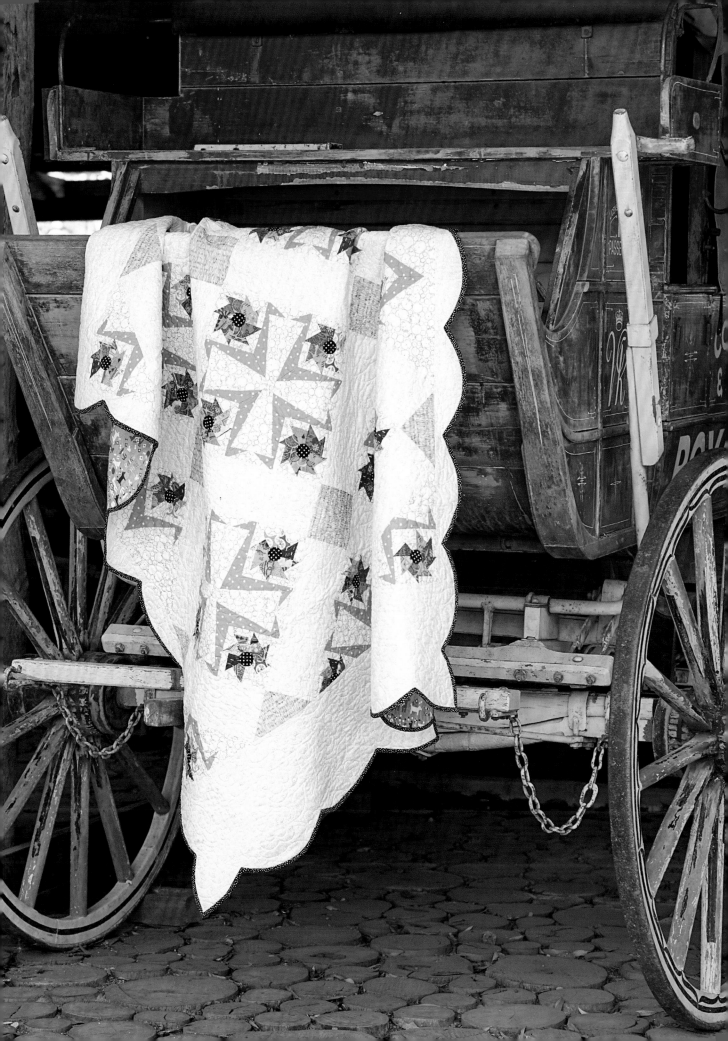

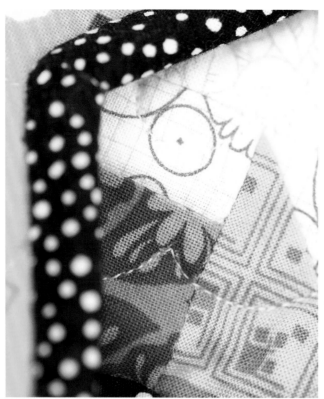

cutting

From the cardboard, cut:
• One Template A (circle)

From the template plastic, cut:
• One Template B (scallop)
• One Template C (corner scallop)

From the eight colored fabrics, cut:
• Thirty 3⅜ in. (8.6 cm) squares from the various fabric. Cross-cut these squares on both diagonals into 120 quarter-square triangles of each fabric.
• Sixty 2½ in. (6.3 cm) squares from the various fabric. Cross-cut these squares on one diagonal into 120 half-square triangles of each fabric.

Tip Be sure to keep your piles of quarter- and half-square triangles separate and labeled.

From the green polka-dot fabric, cut:
• Three 3¼ in. (8.3 cm) strips. Cross-cut these strips into sixty 1¾ x 3¼ in. (4.4 x 8.3 cm) rectangles. Cross-cut half of these rectangles on one diagonal from the top left-hand corner to the bottom right-hand corner, and half from the top right-hand corner to the bottom left-hand corner, for a total of 120 triangles.
• Five 7 in. (17.8 cm) strips. Cross-cut these strips into 120 1½ x 7 in. (3.8 x 17.8 cm) rectangles.

From the black-on-white patterned background fabric, cut:
• Three 3⅜ in. (8.6 cm) strips. Cross-cut these strips into thirty squares. Cross-cut these squares on both diagonals into four quarter-square triangles for 120 quarter-square triangles.
• Four 3⅛ in. (7.9 cm) strips. Cross-cut these strips into 120 1⅛ x 3⅛ in. (2.9 x 7.9 cm) rectangles.
• Four 6½ in. (16.5 cm) strips. Cross-cut these strips into sixty 2⅝ x 6½ in. (6.7 x 16.5 cm) rectangles.
• Three 3¼ in. (8.3 cm) strips. Cross-cut these strips into sixty 3¼ x 1¾ in. (8.3 x 4.4 cm) rectangles. Cross-cut half of these rectangles on one diagonal from the top left-hand corner to the bottom right-hand corner, and half from the top right-hand corner to the bottom left-hand corner, for a total of 120 triangles.
• One 5⅝ in. (14.3 cm) strip. Cross-cut this strip into four squares. Cross-cut these squares on one diagonal for eight half-square triangles.
• One 11 in. (27.9 cm) square. Cross-cut this square on both diagonals for four quarter-square triangles.

From the black-on-white patterned sashing/border fabric, cut:
• Six 5 in. (12.7 cm) strips. Cross-cut these strips into sixteen 5 x 13½ in. (12.7 x 34.3 cm) rectangles for sashing strips.
• Three 3½ in. (8.9 cm) strips for side borders
• Three 10½ in. (26.6 cm) strips for top borders

From black-and-white patterned cornerstone fabric, cut:
• One 5 in. (12.7 cm) strip. Cross-cut this strip into four squares for cornerstones.
• One 8¼ in. (21 cm) strip. Cross-cut this strip into two squares. Cross-cut these squares on two diagonals to make eight quarter-square triangles for cornerstone triangles.

From the white-on-black polka-dot fabric, cut:
• Thirty-two Template A for circles

From the black-and-white polka-dot fabric, cut:
• 2½ in. (6.3 cm) bias strips to measure 10 yd (9.2 m) for binding

making the quilt

sewing

Pinwheels

1. Sew a background-fabric quarter-square triangle to each of the colored quarter-square triangles along the bias edge (see Diagram 1). Press toward the colored fabric. Make 120.

2. Sew a 1¾ x 3¼ in. (4.4 x 8.3 cm) background-fabric rectangle to the bottom of each colored half-square triangle, with the straight ends matching and one end of the background fabric sticking out past the triangle point, and then trim the background-fabric rectangle to the triangle angle (see Diagram 2). Press toward the colored fabric. Make 120.

3. Sew a half-square and a quarter-square unit together to make a square, and then sew a half-square and a quarter-square triangle unit to either side of the square (see Diagram 3). Press the block, taking care not to stretch the bias edges. Make thirty units in this orientation. Make thirty units in the reverse orientation (see Diagram 4).

Leaves

4. Sew the green polka-dot and black-on-white patterned background-fabric triangles of the same size into pairs along the diagonal edges. Trim off the "ears" (see Diagram 5). Press toward the green fabric, taking care not to stretch the bias edges. Make sixty rectangle units, with thirty of the triangles pointing to the right and thirty to the left.

5. Sew one of these rectangles to the top of each 2⅝ x 6½ in. (6.7 x 16.5 cm) background rectangle (see Diagram 6).

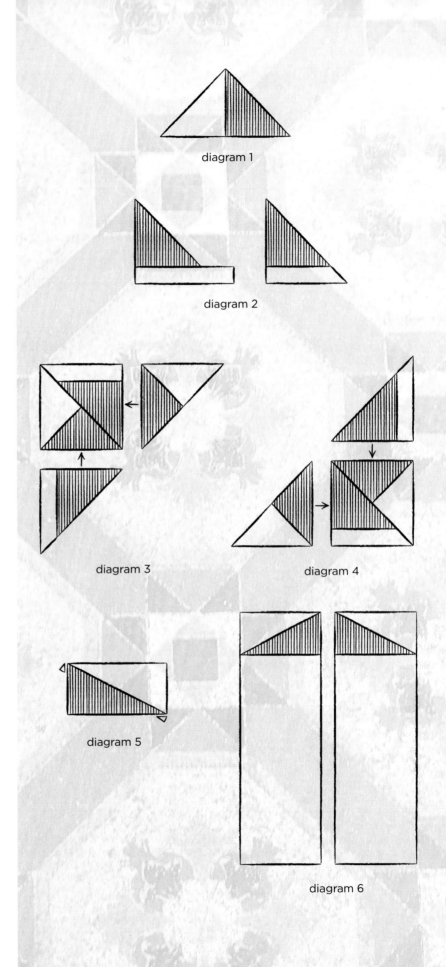

diagram 1

diagram 2

diagram 3

diagram 4

diagram 5

diagram 6

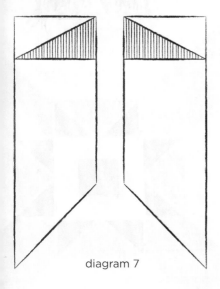

diagram 7

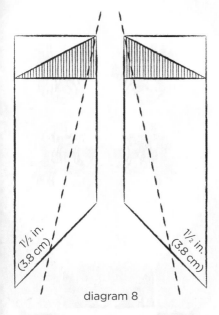

1½ in. (3.8 cm)   1½ in. (3.8 cm)

diagram 8

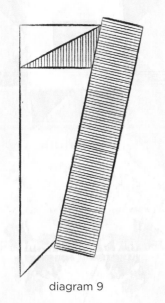

diagram 9

6. On the bottom of these units, trim at a 45-degree angle from the bottom corner of the rectangle. For the left-hand units, trim from the bottom left-hand corner up, and for the right-hand units, trim from the bottom right-hand corner (see Diagram 7).

7. Measure 1½ in. (3.8 cm) from the bottom point along the bias edge that you cut, and make a mark with a pencil. Position your ruler at this mark to the top corner of the leaf at a diagonal angle, and trim as shown by the dotted line (see Diagram 8).

8. Place a 1½ x 7 in. (3.8 x 17.8 cm) green polka-dot rectangle along this cut, with the edges hanging over each end (see Diagram 9). Sew and then press the seam toward the green fabric. Trim the green fabric to match the block (see Diagram 10). Make thirty right-oriented units and thirty left-oriented units.

assembly

9. Sew a left-hand green leaf unit to a left-hand half-pinwheel block with the angles matching, and then repeat for a right-hand green leaf unit and right-hand half-pinwheel block (see Diagram 11).

10. Sew the two halves along the middle to make a pinwheel-and-leaf unit. Make twenty-eight full pinwheel-and-leaf units. The four halves that remain are for the top and bottom triangles.

11. Make thirty-two white-on-black polka-dot circles using Template A following the instructions on page 128 and appliqué the circles in the center of the pinwheels, including the four half-pinwheel-and-leaf units.

12. Sew four pinwheel-and-leaf units together with the leaves pointing inward to make a full block (see Diagram 12). Make five of these blocks.

13. Sew a quarter-square triangle cut from the 11 in. (27.9 cm) background-fabric square to either side of a pinwheel-and-leaf unit (see Diagram 13). Make two of these for the side triangles.

14. Sew a half pinwheel-and-leaf unit to either side of a full pinwheel-and-leaf unit (see Diagram 14). Make two of these for the top and bottom triangles.

15. For the four corner blocks, sew a half-square triangle cut from the 5⅝ in. (14.3 cm) background-fabric squares to either side of the four remaining pinwheel-and-leaf units. The bias edges of the triangles will be facing toward the bottom of the block and will be shorter than the block itself. Trim the bottom of the block to match, including the bottom "V" of the leaves (see Diagram 15).

16. Referring to the quilt photograph, arrange all the units and sashing strips in diagonal rows on your design wall or work surface (see Tip on page 126), starting at the top left-hand corner with a corner block. The second row is a sashing strip with a cornerstone triangle at each end. The third row is a side triangle, a sashing strip, a full block, a sashing strip, and a top triangle, and so on (see Diagram 16). Pin and then sew all the units into diagonal rows, pressing the seams to one side. Pin and then sew the rows together, taking care to match seams where necessary. Press the seams toward the sashing strips.

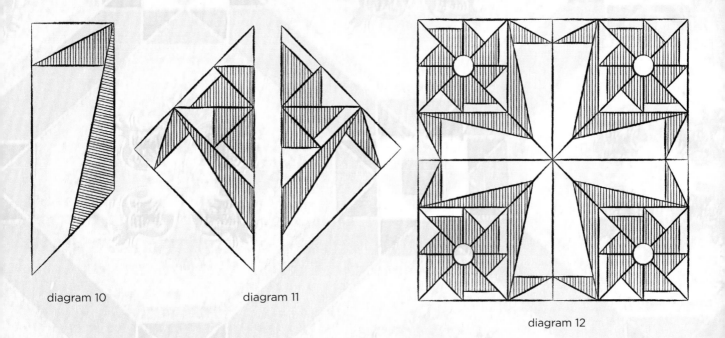

diagram 10

diagram 11

diagram 12

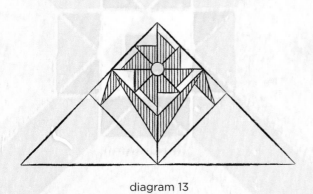
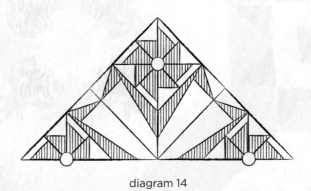

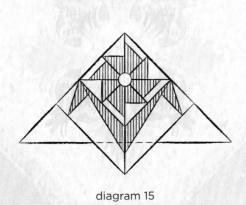

diagram 13

diagram 14

diagram 15

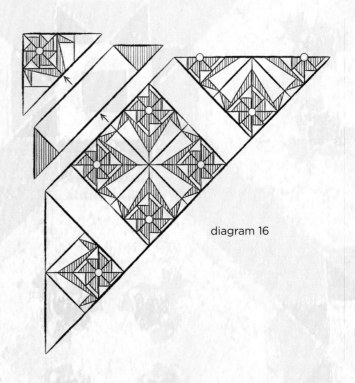

diagram 16

borders

17. Sew the 3½ in. (8.9 cm) black-on-white patterned sashing strips end-to-end to make one long strip. Measure your quilt top through the center from top to bottom. From the long strip, cut two side border strips to this measurement.

18. Fold the strips in half and mark the centers with pins. Mark the sides of the quilt top in the same way. Matching the pins, the ends, and with right sides together, pin the border strips to the quilt top, pinning the length of the borders to keep the borders flat. Sew the borders in place and then press the seams toward the border.

19. Sew the 10½ in. (26.6 cm) black-on-white patterned sashing strips end-to-end to make one long strip. Measure your quilt top through the center from side to side. From the long strip, cut two border strips to this measurement.

20. In the same way, pin and then sew the border strips to the top and bottom of the quilt.

backing, quilting, and binding

21. Cut the backing fabric crosswise into two 63 in. (160 cm) pieces. Remove the selvages and sew the pieces together along the long edges to make the backing. Press the seam open and press the backing.

22. Layer the backing, batting (wadding), and quilt top, following the instructions on page 131. If you are going to have the quilt professionally machine-quilted, do not layer it.

23. Quilt as desired. Mine was professionally machine-quilted in an all-over leafy pattern.

24. Find the center of Template B and line it up with the point of the center flower at the side of the quilt, with the arc of the template touching the outside of the border (the outer edge of the quilt). With a pencil, trace around the arc. Move the template to the left, match the bottom points, and again line the top of the arc up with the edge of the quilt and trace

around the arc. Continue to do this along each edge of the quilt until you reach the corners and there is a space where the full template will no longer fit. Use Template C to trace the corner shapes.

25. At this stage, you have a choice. Many tutorials recommend that you don't trim the quilt top until after you have sewn the binding to the scalloped edge, but I prefer to trim the quilt top and then attach the binding. (If you have never attached binding to a scalloped edge before, I recommend that, before starting, you watch some of the excellent video tutorials on scalloped quilt binding that are available on the internet.) Join the bias binding strips to make a long strip, following the instructions on page 129. Bind the quilt, following the instructions on page 133, but miter the corners at each "V" intersection of the scallops and the points of the corners.

pretty pinwheel

Well, it's certainly not masculine! But who could resist such a pretty combination of appliqué and piecing for a little girl's quilt? The checked background provides a charming setting for the scalloped frame. It's like a picture of a favorite childhood memory.

This quilt could easily be used as a block for a larger quilt. Four of these blocks together with a border would make a queen-size quilt, or one block in the center would be the start of a lovely medallion quilt.

finished size

Crib (cot) size quilt, 43½ in. (110.5 cm) wide x 53½ in. (135.9 cm) long

Note All strips are cut across the width of the fabric from fold to selvage, and seams are stitched with right sides together using a ¼ in. (6 mm) seam allowance unless otherwise stated.

material requirements

- 1 yd (1 m) natural linen for center
- 6 in. (16 cm) blue patterned fabric for pinwheel
- 6 in. (16 cm) red patterned fabric for pinwheel
- 6 in. (16 cm) black-and-white checked fabric for circle and pinwheel stick
- One fat quarter of green patterned fabric for appliqué ribbon, or 2 yd (2 m) readymade bias tape
- 1 yd (1 m) black-and-white polka-dot fabric for frame and binding
- 1½ yd (1.4 m) pink-and-white checked linen for background
- 3 yd (2.8 cm) backing fabric
- 50 x 60 in. (127 x 153 cm) piece cotton batting (wadding)
- Hera marker
- Piece of thin cardboard (see page 140 for templates)
- Aluminum foil

- Several sheets of newspaper
- Scissors for cutting paper
- Fabric scissors
- Cotton thread for piecing
- Silver gel pen
- Appliqué glue
- Straw needles for appliqué
- Cotton thread to match appliqué fabrics
- Small, sharp scissors for trimming appliqué
- Masking tape for marking quilting lines
- Crewel embroidery needles no. 9 for hand quilting
- Perle 8 cotton in light pink and black for quilting
- Rotary cutter, mat, and ruler
- Sewing machine
- General sewing supplies

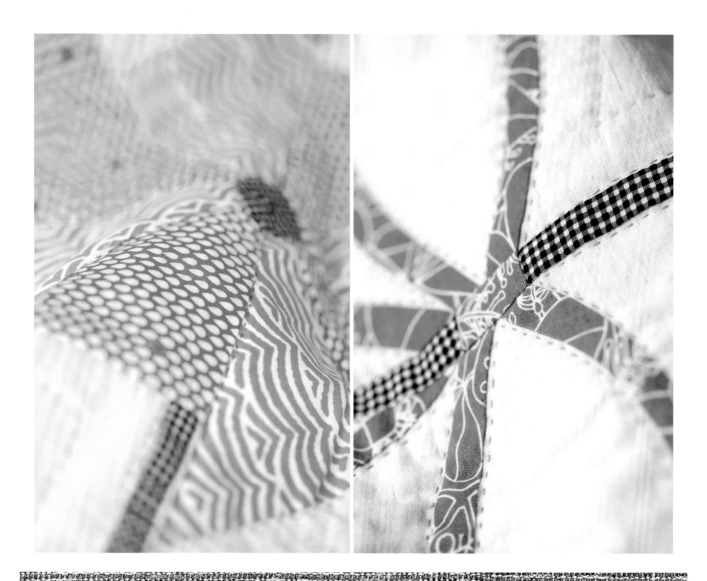

cutting

From the cardboard, cut:
• One Template A (circle)

From the newspaper, cut:
• One full Template B (frame). To do this, tape several sheets of newspaper together until you have a piece large enough for the frame. Fold the newspaper into quarters and trace the enlarged template onto one quarter of the newspaper, with the edges along the fold where indicated. Cut out the template through all four layers for a full frame. Cut out the center of the frame.

From the plain linen, cut:
• One 2½ in. (6.3 cm) strip. Cross-cut this strip into four 8 in. (20.4 cm) lengths.
• One 5⅞ in. (14.9 cm) strip. Cross-cut this strip into two squares. Cross-cut these squares on one diagonal into four half-square triangles.
• Two 6½ in. (16.5 cm) strips.

From the blue patterned fabric, cut:
• One 5⅞ in. (14.9 cm) strip. Cross-cut this strip into two squares. Cross-cut these squares on one diagonal into four half-square triangles.

From the red patterned fabric, cut:
• One 5⅞ in. (14.9 cm) strip. Cross-cut this strip into two squares. Cross-cut these squares on one diagonal into four half-square triangles.

From the black-and-white checked fabric, cut:
• One Template A
• One 1 x 24 in. (2.5 x 61 cm) strip for pinwheel stick

From the green patterned fabric, cut:
• Four 1 in. (2.5 cm) bias strips for bow, following the instructions on page 129.

From the black-and-white polka-dot fabric, cut:
• One Template B for frame, following the instructions on page 127
• Six 3 in. (7.6 cm) strips for binding

From the pink-and-white checked linen, cut:
• One 43½ x 53½ in. (110.5 x 136 cm) piece

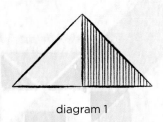

diagram 1

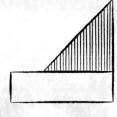

diagram 2

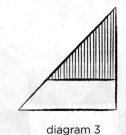

diagram 3

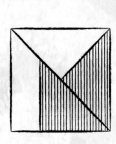

diagram 4

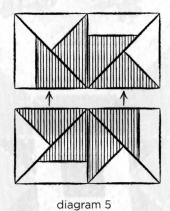

diagram 5

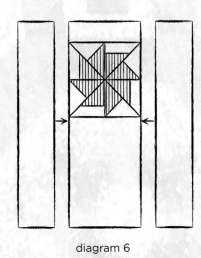

diagram 6

making the quilt
sewing and assembly

1. Sew a linen half-square triangle to each of the blue patterned half-square triangles along one of the edges adjacent to the 90-degree angle (see Diagram 1). Press toward the blue fabric.

2. Sew an 8 x 2½ in. (20.4 x 6.3 cm) linen strip to the bottom of each red patterned triangle, with the straight ends matching and one end of the linen sticking out past the triangle point (see Diagram 2). Trim the linen to the triangle angle (see Diagram 3). Press toward the red fabric.

3. Sew a red and a blue triangle unit together to make a square (see Diagram 4). Press the seam to one side. Make four squares.

4. Referring to the quilt photograph on page 123, arrange the four squares together to form a pinwheel (see Diagram 5) on your design wall or work surface (see Tip on page 126). Be careful to orient the triangles in the correct way to form the pattern. Pin and then sew the pieces together.

5. Press the block, taking care not to stretch the bias edges, and measure it through the center. It should measure 14¼ in. (36.2 cm). From the remaining plain linen, cut one strip to this width and cross-cut into one 4 in. (10.2 cm) piece and one 21 in. (53.3 cm) piece. Sew the 4 in. (10.2 cm) piece to the top of the block, and the 21 in. (53.3 cm) piece to the bottom of the block (see Diagram 6). Press the seams toward the linen.

6. Measure your piece through the center from top to bottom. It should measure 38¼ in. (97.3 cm). Cut the two 6½ in. (16.5 cm) strips of linen to this length. Fold the strips in half and mark the centers with pins. Mark the sides of the quilt top in the same way. Matching the pins, the ends, and with right sides together, pin the strips to the sides of the quilt top, pinning along the length of the strips to keep the strips flat. Sew the strips in place and then press the seams toward the linen (see Diagram 6).

appliqué

Pinwheel

7. Make a black-and-white checked circle using Template A following the instructions on page 128 and appliqué the circle in the center of the pinwheel.

8. For the pinwheel stick, use a Hera marker to score a line ¼ in. (6 mm) from the edge of each long side of the 1 x 24 in. (2.5 x 61 cm) black-and-white checked strip. Press the edges underneath along the scoring lines.

9. Fold the quilt top and press a crease from approximately ½ in. (12 mm) inside the point of the bottom blue triangle to the bottom of the quilt (see Diagram 7).

10. Place the black-and-white checked strip along the pressed crease and secure it with dots of glue. Unpick the seam a little where the strip meets the red patterned triangle and push the end of the strip inside.

11. Make bias strips for the appliqué bow from the green patterned fabric, following the instructions on page 129.

12. Using a window or a light box and a chalk pencil, trace the enlarged ribbon appliqué layout diagram (on page 140) onto the linen background, with the top of the center knot of the bow 16½ in. (42 cm) from the bottom of the block. You will only need a single line as a guide for where to place the bias strips.

13. Using your iron to help curve the strips, place bias pieces, cut to size, over the drawn lines. Glue them in place, ensuring you do not glue the ends of the strips because you will have to turn them under for a neat finish.

14. Appliqué the ribbon in place following the instructions on pages 127–128, and then appliqué the pinwheel pole in place. Appliqué the open seam over the strip.

Frame

15. Center the black-and-white polka-dot frame over the linen piece, ensuring you have enough linen under the frame at the top and bottom to allow for appliqué along the inside of the frame. Carefully lift the edges of the inside of the frame and place dots of glue at least ¼ in. (6 mm) inside the sewing line to secure.

16. When the glue has dried (after about two minutes), finger-press around the gel pen line of the frame and appliqué it to the linen background. Turn the quilt top over and carefully trim away the excess background fabric from behind the frame, ¼ in. (6 mm) from the stitching line.

17. Press the 43½ x 53½ in. (110.5 x 135.9 cm) pink-and-white checked piece and the quilt top into quarters. Trim the excess black-and-white polka-dot fabric away from the outside scallops of the frame, ¼ in. (6 mm) from the drawn line.

18. Center the frame on the pink checked background using the pressed creases as guides. Carefully lift the edges of the frame and use spots of glue to secure it. Appliqué the outside edge of the frame to the pink-and-white checked fabric. Turn it to the back and trim the excess pink-and-white checked fabric from behind the frame and the center piece.

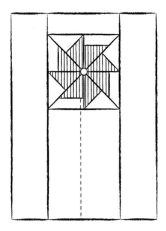

diagram 7

backing, quilting, and binding

19. Cut the backing fabric crosswise into two 54 in. (137 cm) pieces. Remove the selvages and sew the pieces together along the long edges to make the backing. Press the seam allowance open and press the backing.

20. Layer the backing, batting (wadding), and quilt top, following the instructions on page 131.

21. Using Aurifil Mako' Ne 12 weight black cotton, outline-quilt around the pinwheel, stick, and ribbon, and the inside and outside edges of the scalloped frame. Using light pink thread, quilt a grid pattern on the pink-and-white checked background fabric, following the lines of the checked pattern.

22. Bind the quilt, following the instructions on page 133.

fabrics

Today you can find a wonderful selection of patchwork prints that absolutely cry out to be made into quilts. I like to give them even more impact by mixing them with solids, more unusual prints, and vintage fabrics that add interesting textures and visual movement. In particular, in keeping with this book's theme of vintage quilts, I wanted to use as many old fabrics as I could. They aren't always prominent—they are just mixed in with modern patchwork fabrics—but they work wonderfully to bring texture, dimension, and a little nostalgia to a quilt.

Patchwork prints

These are widely available by the yard (meter) or in smaller pieces known as fat quarters and fat eighths (see page 154), often in bundles of fabrics that are the same weight and that coordinate in color and pattern.

Low-volume fabric

These fabrics are light in color and sparse in print. They are generally used for a background or to make a quilt very light and open in tone.

Solids

There are so many ranges of solids on the market now, and bundles of rainbow colors are readily available. Some of the quilts in this book incorporate several tones of the same color, and some feature solids in rainbows of tones. When I use solids, I tend to choose something with a bit of texture rather than a flat solid fabric, which, to my eye, creates a "hole" in the quilt, or a space that stops your eye moving. The fabrics I use as solids are often linen or shot cotton so that they still have some depth of movement and shape.

Japanese fabrics

I love to incorporate fabrics in interesting and unusual colors, and odd prints or novelty prints, especially small animals! Nearly every quilt I have ever made has a little animal in it somewhere. My favorite source of these fabrics is Japan, where their love of all things cute matches my own. Lots of patchwork shops stock at least a small range of interesting modern Japanese prints, and many online shops have entire sections devoted to them.

Feedsacks

These fabrics come from exactly where their name suggests—they were once sacks! From around the 1850s, improvements in factories, fabrics, and sewing machines meant that the transportation of goods such as flour, seed, sugar, animal feed, hams, and even sausages was done in machine-sewn bags. At a time when fabric was expensive and money was tight, enterprising women soon realized that the fabric of the sacks was just as valuable as the contents. The sacks printed with company logos and the like were often soaked and scrubbed to remove the ink as much as possible, and then used for men's underwear. The manufacturers discovered that printing the sacks with designs for calendars and tea towels would improve sales, and women soon were sending their husbands off to the store for the right sack to complete their set. Eventually factories began producing printed fabrics, and if the sacks were popular and sold well, the prints were produced as yardage and used for dresses and shirts.

Vintage sheets

As a child of the 1970s, I remember so clearly the wonderful prints on my bedsheets and pillowcases. Clearly I'm not the only one, as vintage sheets from the 1950s onward are available all over the place at present! The fun and funky designs and delicate crisp florals are wonderful for quilt-making. However, be cautious about quality and polyester content. Also, I wouldn't recommend backing a quilt for hand-quilting with a sheet, no matter now tempting the pattern, as the sheeting fabric is often tightly woven and difficult to needle.

Recycled fabrics

Fabric recycled from old cotton or linen clothing is in the true spirit of patchwork: make do and mend. There are beautiful prints and lovely textures to be gleaned from thrift shops and even your own closet. There are also companies online that salvage old clothes and linens, wash and deconstruct them, and sell them for patchwork in squares and strips.

Vintage fabrics

Finding vintage fabric is not difficult! You can use old clothing, sheets, and fabrics purchased from patchwork shops, thrift stores, or estate sales— in the Resources section (page 156) there is a list of some of the ones I like to frequent. If you have older family members or friends who sew, their stashes might also be a wonderful place to find fabrics from another era.

I love to sew with vintage and antique fabrics, but there are a few things you need to know before you jump in—they need some love and care first.

1. Inspect the fabric as best you can for holes and stains (difficult if buying online). A stain near the edge can be cut away but a big stain right in the middle of the main print might not be so easy!

2. Check the fiber content. I use nothing but natural fibers in my quilts—100 percent cotton or linen. If you can't tell what the fabric is just by touch or by a clothing label, cut a small piece off and set it on fire (carefully!). If the fabric shrivels like a piece of plastic, then it has a synthetic-fiber content. Ironing with a hot iron can also reveal a fabric's secrets—either the fabric will shrivel under the iron, or you will get that "polyester" smell from the heated fabric.

3. Always, always, always wash! Vintage and antique fabrics can fall apart easily during washing, or the colors can run, or they may shrink. If the fabric is from old clothing, you don't know that the garment was washed before it was sold or put away, and there may be sweat or makeup stains that can become more prominent with age. Treat the fabric just as you would a normal cotton or linen, or how you would want to treat your finished quilt. There is no point spending hours piecing or hand appliquéing if you then find the fabric you have used is defective. I wash all my old fabrics with a wool wash or a product like Soak, just in the washing machine on a normal cold cycle. If you are worried the fabric will fray, place it in a lingerie bag before washing. If you have a very delicate old feedsack or something that you want to use for a piece that won't get much handling, I would recommend hand-washing it and drying it flat in the sun.

4. When you come to use your fabric, be mindful of its imperfections. If there are holes or stains you want to avoid, putting a circle around them in pencil or putting a pin at the spot can help you to remember not to blithely cut and piece the holes into your quilt. Many vintage and antique fabrics are also a looser weave than their modern counterparts—take care with the grain line when cutting and pressing to avoid stretching and puckering.

tools and threads

Tools I use that are essential
• Sewing machine in good working order (unless you are a dedicated hand sewer!) and replacement needles. I use a Universal sharp, 70/10 needle for all my patchwork.
• ¼ in. (6 mm) machine foot to fit your machine. Do consider investing in one of these—they are a little pricey but will make a huge difference to your stitching and make accurate seams so much easier.
• Dressmaking scissors for cutting fabric only
• Scissors for cutting paper or plastic
• Thread snips or small, sharp scissors
• Seam ripper
• Straight pins
• Tape measure
• Perspex quilter's ruler(s)—it is handy to have two rulers of the same size to assist in cutting strips without having to turn the cutting mat around
• Rotary cutter (the best you can afford) and replacement blades
• Self-healing cutting mat

• Masking tape, for securing backing fabric to a flat surface and for making straight hand-quilting lines without marking your quilt
• Chalk pencil and silver gel pen, for marking curved quilting and appliqué lines
• Quilter's safety pins (if you are pinning quilt layers rather than basting)
• Quilter's hoop, for hand-quilting (this is not an embroidery hoop)
• Quilter's thimble
• Needles for appliqué. I use a Milliner's needle #11 for my appliqué. I like a long, slim, fine needle with a small eye to assist with tiny stitches and easy turning.
• Needles for hand-quilting. I use a crewel embroidery needle #9 for quilting with perle cotton or Aurifil Mako' Ne 12 weight cotton. You need a long, sturdy needle that isn't too thick, with a small eye.
• Liquid appliqué glue, such as Roxanne or Patchwork With Busy Fingers. This is washable, acid-free glue made especially for appliqué. I do not ever use glue sticks for appliqué.

Tools I use that are nice to have
• Hera marker—for making bias tape using my method (see page 129) and for marking quilting lines or lines for vines without using a pen or pencil
• Fine patchwork pins—more expensive than regular pins, but so slim and fine that they allow pinning without puckering of fabric
• Needle rest—contains a magnet that allows you to lay down your needle without putting it through your work
• Wonder clips—I use these little marvels for everything from holding down a binding to English paper piecing. They are also very useful for keeping cut pieces and stack of blocks together.
• Turning tool—something with a long, pointy end can be invaluable for helping to feed points under your machine foot cleanly. I also use mine often to help sweep under tight curves when appliquéing. There are many tools on the market for this; I have a beautiful porcupine quill given to me by a quilting friend.
• A door peeper, easily and cheaply bought from a hardware store, can be invaluable for seeing your blocks from a distance, which helps you balance tone, color, and scale.

specialty rulers

All the quilts in this book can be made using a standard 24 in. (60 cm) quilter's ruler and the templates provided. You could also use a specialty ruler made for cutting diamonds, half-square and quarter-square triangles, and 60-degree triangles. Although I have not usually listed them in the requirements for each project, these rulers make cutting much quicker and easier—if you wish to use them, by all means do so. They are usually sold with detailed instructions for their use and are widely available from your local patchwork shop, or from me.

Half-square triangle ruler
A half-square ruler, also called a 45-degree triangle ruler, is useful but not strictly necessary for cutting half-square triangles. You can, of course, cut these triangles using a standard quilter's ruler by cross-cutting strips into squares, then cross-cutting each square in half on one diagonal, resulting in two half-square triangles. The size of the square that you cut when cutting half-square triangles in this way should always be ⅞ in. (2.2 cm) larger than the desired finished size of the triangle.

Specialized half-square triangle rulers, however, have already allowed for the seam allowance at the point of the triangle, thus eliminating the "ears" on the seam. This means

that if you are using a half-square triangle ruler, you will cut the triangles from a strip of fabric rather than from squares, and the size of your strip should be only ½ in. (12 mm) larger than the desired finished size of the triangle, not ⅞ in. (2.2 cm). The half-square triangles you cut with this ruler will have a blunt point for easy alignment and will require less trimming.

A half-square or quarter-square triangle ruler (which works similarly but allows cutting with the bias in the correct position) can be used to cut the triangles in Centenary, Ebb and Flow, Mosaic, Ink Pink, Keep It Down, Planting, and Pretty Pinwheel.

60-degree triangle ruler
This ruler is used primarily to cut equilateral triangles (each internal angle is 60 degrees and all three sides are the same length) but it is also useful for accurately cutting diamonds, half-diamonds, and 30-degree triangles. I used this ruler for Flash and Spark.

Perspex ruler sets are available that are suitable for several of the quilts in this book; please see page 157 for details.

threads

Match the thread to the fabric when piecing. For example, when using cotton fabric, use cotton thread. Avoid using polyester thread for patchwork—over time, the threads will wear differently and the polyester thread will cut through the fibers of the cotton.

Always use a fine, good-quality thread for your sewing machine. Your machine will produce less fluff sewing with good-quality material, and your seams will lie flatter and last longer.

In most situations, cream, white, or gray threads are appropriate for piecing—there is no need to change colors to match the fabrics you are sewing. If you are using a multicolored fabric, use a neutral-colored thread, such as beige or gray, which will blend into the background.

For appliqué I use 50 weight cotton thread, which is very fine and helps to hide your stitches. For hand-quilting, I use perle 8 cotton or Aurifil Mako' Ne 12 weight cotton rather than traditional quilting thread. I like my stitches to stand out and make a statement, and I love the decorative element that thicker thread adds to the quilt. A thicker thread is much easier for beginners to handle because you can take larger stitches—up to ¼ in. (6 mm) in length—and you use a longer, thicker needle than for traditional quilting.

techniques

This section covers the principal techniques used in this book. Some are techniques you may never have tried before, while others are techniques that I might attack a little differently than you are accustomed to. Therefore, make sure you read this section carefully before starting your quilt.

half-square triangles

There are different ways to cut and piece half-square triangles, such as using a 45-degree ruler, or ruling diagonal lines on a pair of squares and then sewing ¼ in. (6 mm) both sides of the line and finally cutting along the line. However, the projects in this book are written using the most common technique for half-square triangles, which is to cut a square and cut the square on one diagonal into two triangles. The triangles are then sewn into pairs along the diagonals using ¼ in. (6 mm) seams.

As a result, the cutting instructions include ⅞ in. (2.2 cm) for the seams of half-square triangles. For example, if 2⅞ in. (7.3 cm) squares are cut into half-square triangles that are then joined in pairs, the finished size of each half-square unit will be 2 in. (5.1 cm). If you use a different cutting technique, ensure that you cut the pieces to the correct size.

Because the diagonal edges are on the bias, they will be prone to stretching when being pressed, making the quilt out of shape, so take care when pressing them.

seams

Unless otherwise instructed, the seams in this book are stitched with right sides together using a ¼ in. (6 mm) seam allowance.

Sewing partial seams

There are times when a quilt cannot be put together in straight lines. Because of the step-downs or corner meeting places in the pattern, it cannot be sewn together in rows. Instead, a seam is left partially open and then is closed later, after further pieces have been sewn on. The partial-seam technique is used in Centenary (see pages 64–65, steps 13, 14, and 18) and Ink Pink (see pages 104–106, steps 3–5). If you find this technique difficult, you may wish to look at my video class at www.craftsy.com.

Tip You need a big, flat, clean surface on which to arrange the patchwork or appliqué, to help you balance the color. I recommend you use a design wall made from a piece of batting (wadding) or a flannel sheet pinned to the wall or a window, which allows you to step back and view the design at a distance. Alternatively, you can use the floor or a bed.

1. To close the partial seam, first sew the red square to the green square along its length.

2. Now close the seam along the length of the rectangle, as shown.

appliqué

There are various appliqué techniques, but my favorite is my needle-turn method, described below. Whatever method you choose, complete all the appliqué before you piece the blocks together, unless otherwise instructed.

All the quilts in this book are suited to machine appliqué. If you wish to machine-appliqué your quilts, remove the seam allowance from around each shape before you cut it out.

Before beginning the appliqué, decide where you want your shapes to sit on the background block. Use a sharp 2B pencil or other marker to lightly trace the shapes onto the background fabric. A light box is useful when tracing; if you don't have one, tape the design to be traced onto a sunny window, lightly tape the fabric over it, and then trace the design.

Remember that some designs need to have their elements sewn down in a particular order. For example, when sewing a flower, the stem needs to be sewn first so that it sits under the flower petals, then the petals added, and finally the flower center and the leaves. If you are working on a complicated appliqué design and you think you might get confused, draw or photocopy a diagram of the complete design, determine the order in which the pieces need to be laid down, and then number the shapes on the diagram so that you can keep track.

Needle-turn appliqué

1. Using a sharp 2B pencil, trace the template shapes onto template plastic or cardstock. Using paper scissors (not your fabric scissors), cut along the traced line.

2. Place the template on the right side of the fabric and trace around it, taking care to leave space between the pieces for a seam allowance. I use a silver gel pen for marking sewing lines, first, because it's reflective and shows up on any fabric, and second, because it's really easy to see whether you have turned your shape under neatly. If you can still see silver, you haven't got the shape right! However, gel pen does not wash off. Once you have traced your shape onto the fabric, you're married to it, so be careful with that tracing!

3. Cut the shapes out a scant ¼ in. (6 mm) from the gel line. Finger-press along the line all around the shape, including into any curves or points. Don't be tempted to iron the seam in; a finger-pressed line is easy to manipulate, whereas an ironed line is difficult to change if you iron a point into a crease or a line in the wrong spot (not to mention the fact that you'd be very likely to burn your fingers!). Finger-pressing is a guide to help you turn the fabric as you sew.

4. Position the pieces on the background block, using the traced outline or photograph supplied with the pattern as a guide. Dotted lines on the templates indicate which parts of each piece should be placed under adjacent pieces.

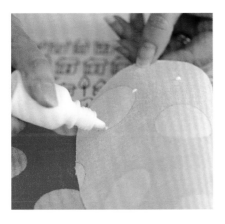

5. Instead of pins, I use appliqué glue to fix the pieces temporarily onto the background. You can glue all the appliqué shapes onto a quilt and carry it around with you, without worrying that the pins have come out. You only need a few dots of glue on each shape to make them stick. Leave for a few minutes for the glue to dry. Don't worry if the glue smudges, as it is easily peeled back later or washed off.

6. Thread your appliqué needle with thread to match the appliqué fabric. Always match your appliqué thread to the color of the fabric shape that you are appliquéing, not to the background. I use very long, fine straw needles for appliqué—the finer the needle, the smaller you can make your stitches for invisible appliqué. You can start anywhere, but try not to start on an inside curve or a point.

7. Tie a knot in the thread and come up from the back to the front of the background fabric, catching the very edge of the appliqué shape with your needle, as shown.

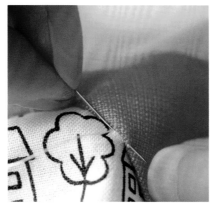

8. Go down into the background fabric right next to where you came up, run your needle along underneath the background, and come up again on the edge of the appliqué shape, as shown. Don't try to turn the whole edge under before you sew it; just turn under the small section you are working on. This makes it easier to keep track of the gel-pen line and make sure that you turn it all under.

9. Sew all around the cut edge of the appliqué shape in this manner. Your stitches should just catch the edge of the fabric and be small and close together, which will make the appliqué strong and avoid it being torn or looking puckered. Continue until you have sewn all around the outside of the shape and then tie the thread off at the back with a small knot.

10. Turn the block over and make a small cut at the back of the shape, taking care not to cut the appliqué. Cut away the background fabric underneath the appliqué. Be sure not to cut closer than ¼ in. (6 mm) away from the seam lines. Although it is not necessary, removing the fabric in this way makes the appliqué sit nicely and creates fewer layers to quilt through, especially where appliqué pieces overlap. Repeat this process with each shape. Remove the background from under each piece before you apply the next one.

Perfect appliqué circles

Turning a perfect circle can be difficult with hand appliqué. An easy method for turning the circles is to use a cardstock or Mylar template and aluminum foil.

1. Cut a cardstock or Mylar circle to the size you want the finished circle to be. Trace the circle onto the back of the fabric using a pencil, and cut the circle out a generous ¼ in. (6 mm) outside the traced line. Cut a piece of foil larger than both circles. It does not have to be a perfect circle—a rough shape will do.

2. Place the foil shiny side down on the ironing board first, then the fabric circle right side down, then the cardstock or Mylar circle on top, aligning with the circle you traced. Pull all the edges of the foil up to cover the cardstock circle, pulling the edges in as you do so and smoothing the curve so that you don't have any pointy edges anywhere.

3. Turn the foil circle over to the shiny side and press with the iron. Give the foil a few seconds to cool down, then open the foil up and remove the fabric and the cardstock or Mylar. You now have a perfect circle ready to glue and appliqué to your background fabric.
.

Making a quick bias strip

Bias strips are used in appliqué for making vines or stems for flowers, basket handles, and the like. The strips need to be cut on the bias so that they can be easily ironed and glued into a curve without puckering. Fat quarters are useful for making bias strips for small projects, as they are square and you will get a good length of strip from one square.

1. Using the 45-degree angle line on your patchwork ruler, make a 45-degree cut along one corner of the fabric. Still using this line on the ruler, cut parallel strips from the fabric that are ½ in. (12 mm) wider than you want the finished bias strip to be.

2. To join strips end-to-end, place them with right sides together at right angles to each other and sew on the diagonal until they are as long as you require. Fold back, trim the seam allowances, and press the seams open to reduce bulk when stitching.

3. Using a Hera marker, score a line ¼ in. (6 mm) from the edge on both sides of the strip and all the way along the length, as shown.

4. Iron the edges of the bias strip under on both long edges along the score marks to make bias tape.

Applying bias curves

1. First, mark the line of the bias curve that you want to appliqué lightly on the background fabric with a pencil.

2. Take your bias strips and the background fabric to the ironing board. Put one end of the bias strip on the beginning of the pencil line and put the tip of the iron onto the bias. Pull the bias strip out in front of the iron and slowly begin pressing the strip along the pencil line you made, to press the curve in.

3. If you have a strip longer than the ironing board, iron as far as you can go along the curve and stop. Lift the bias strip up carefully and put dots of glue along the pencil line, then replace the strip and let dry. Shift the background fabric along the ironing board and repeat until you have glued the bias to the background.

Appliqué points and curves

To get a sharp point, first sew all the way up to the point on one side. Now fold the fabric down 90 degrees under the point, and sweep the remaining fabric downward and underneath the main part of the point. Take a stitch right at the point again and give it a sharp tug, then continue sewing down the other side of the point.

When you get to an inside curve, you've reached your next challenge! Although you can sew all around the outside curves without clipping, inside curves need clipping. However, I never clip anything until I am ready to sew it, otherwise it can fray and get messy; therefore, sew all the way up to the curve before you clip. Using very sharp, small scissors, carefully make clips up to the silver-gel line, about ¼ in. (6 mm) apart, all around the inner curve, and then sew the curve right away.

constructing your quilt

If a layout diagram is given, be sure to refer to it as well as to the photograph. Many quilt designs, especially complex ones using more than one type of block, feature optical illusions caused by the way in which the various components are combined. Sometimes the logic of the quilt's construction will not become clear until you look at a layout diagram.

Adding borders

Borders may be added for decorative effect or to increase the quilt's size, or both. They may have squared-off or mitered corners. The quilt pattern will tell you what length to cut the borders, but you should always measure your quilt before cutting the border fabric, and then adjust the length of the border strips if necessary.

To get a true measurement, measure in both directions through the center of the quilt rather than along the edges. This is because the edges may have distorted a little during the making of the quilt, especially if any of the edge pieces are bias-cut. Use these measurements to calculate the length of each border. When pinning them to the quilt top, be sure to pin for the full length of the borders—this is important to keep the borders flat.

Borders with squared-off corners:

On these the side borders will be the length of the quilt top. The top and bottom borders will be the width of the quilt top with the side borders added. Unless a pattern indicates otherwise, sew the side borders on first, press the seams toward the border, then add the top and bottom borders.

Borders with mitered corners: Here, each border will need to be the width or length of the quilt, plus twice the width of the border, to allow enough fabric for mitering, plus seam allowance. Sew each border to the edge of the quilt, beginning and ending the seam a precise 1/4 in. (6 mm) from the edge of the quilt. Fold the quilt so that the side and the top are flush and the two border strips extend to the side. Use your ruler and a 45-degree-angle line to mark a line from the 1/4 in. (6 mm) point to the edge of the strip. Sew

along this line and check before cutting that it will lie flat, then trim off the extra fabric. Repeat for all four corners.

Layering the quilt

Once you have added all the borders, and before you can begin quilting, you need to assemble all three layers of the quilt—the batting (wadding) is sandwiched between the quilt top and the backing.

Types of batting: Some battings need to be quilted closer together than others to stop them from drifting around within the quilt or fragmenting when washed. Polyester batting requires less quilting than cotton or wool batting. However, some polyester battings have a tendency to fight the sewing machine. Wool battings (usually actually a wool/polyester or a wool/cotton blend) provide more warmth and comfort than polyester battings. However, they require more quilting, and those that are not needle-punched tend to pill. Needle-punched wool blends are more stable and require less quilting. Traditional cotton battings require a lot of quilting, as much as every 1/2–3 in. (12mm–7.5 cm). Needle-punched cotton battings are more stable and can be quilted up to 10 in. (25 cm) apart. Ask your quilt store for advice if you are unsure of what to choose.

Making the backing: The batting and backing should be at least 4 in. (10 cm) larger all around than the quilt top. You may need to join two widths of fabric, or add a strip of scraps or leftover blocks, to obtain a large-enough piece for the backing. Press any seams in the backing open to reduce bulk when quilting. If you need to join two pieces of batting, butt them up together without overlapping, and machine-zigzag a seam.

Assembling the layers: Press the quilt top and backing fabric. Lay the backing fabric right side down on a large, flat, clean surface (preferably one that is not carpeted), smooth it out carefully, and then tape it to the surface using masking tape. Tape it at intervals along all sides, but do not tape the corners, as this will cause the bias to stretch out of shape. Place the batting on top of the backing fabric and smooth it out. Center the well-pressed quilt top, right side up, on top of the batting, ensuring that the top and backing are square to each other. Smooth out.

Basting

Once you have assembled the three layers, you need to baste them together ready for quilting. Basting can be done with safety pins (when machine-quilting) or long hand stitches (when hand-quilting).

If you are using safety pins, prior to machine-quilting, start from the center of the quilt and pin through all three layers at intervals of about 8 in. (20 cm). Make sure the pins are kept away from the lines to be quilted. Once the whole quilt is safety-pinned, it can be moved. Do not use safety pins if you are hand-quilting, as the pins prevent the hoop from sitting evenly.

To baste using hand stitches, prior to hand-quilting, baste the whole quilt both horizontally and vertically, always working from the center out, using long hand stitches at intervals of about 6 in. (15 cm). Using a curved needle is a good idea, as this makes the task easier on the wrists. Do not baste using hand stitches if you intend to machine-quilt, as the basting threads will get caught under the presser foot.

Some quilting stores offer a machine-basting service. This can be a worthwhile investment, especially if you are going to be doing fine hand-quilting in the traditional manner, a task that can take many months or even years.

Remove the basting stitches or safety pins only once all the quilting is complete.

quilting

Quilting can be fairly rudimentary, with its main purpose being to hold together the layers of the quilt, or it can be decorative and sometimes extremely elaborate. Machine-quilting is quick, but nothing beats hand-quilting for sheer heirloom beauty and a soft hand to the finished quilt.

Designs for hand-quilting, or elaborate designs for machine-quilting, are generally marked on the quilt top before the quilt's layers are sandwiched together. On pale fabrics, the marking is done lightly in pencil or chalk pencil; on dark fabrics, a special quilter's silver pencil or chalk pencil is used. Pencil lines can be erased later. Be very light and cautious with your marking, because even pencil can be difficult to remove.

Free-flowing lines can be drawn on, but if you intend to quilt straight lines or a cross-hatched design masking tape can be used to mark out the lines on the quilt top. Such tape comes in various widths, from $\frac{1}{4}$ in. (6 mm) upward.

If you intend to outline-quilt by machine, you may be able to sew straight-enough lines by eye; if not, you will need to mark the quilt top first, or use your machine foot as a guide.

Hand-quilting

Quilting by hand produces a softer line than machine-quilting and will add to the lovingly handmade quality of a quilt. Most of the quilts in this book are quilted using Aurifil Mako' Ne 12 weight cotton or perle cotton, since these are often easier for beginners to work with and stand out vividly against the fabric's surface. However, traditional waxed quilting thread can be used if you prefer.

To quilt by hand, the fabric needs to be held in a frame (also known as a quilting hoop). Freestanding frames are available, but hand-held ones are cheaper, more portable, and

Machine-quilting

You may want to machine-quilt your quilt yourself, in which case you could take a class at your local quilt shop or online. However, I use and recommend a professional quilting service for a couple of good reasons. First, finished quilts are usually quite large and, consequently, rather cumbersome. It is a fairly tricky job to manipulate the bulk of the quilt on a domestic sewing machine, even using a specialized walking foot. Having pieced your precious quilt so carefully, it would be a shame to spoil it now with puckers and distortions. Second, professional machine-quilters offer a large range of quilting patterns to suit every need and taste and can also advise you on a design that will enhance all your careful work.

just as effective. One edge of a hand-held frame can be rested against a table or bench to free up both hands.

Hand-quilting, like machine-quilting, should commence in the center of the quilt and proceed outward. Place the plain (inner) ring of the frame under the center of the quilt. Position the other ring, with the screw, over the top of the quilt to align with the inner ring. Tighten the screw so that the fabric in the frame becomes firm, but not drum-tight.

For traditional quilting, choose the smallest needle that you feel comfortable with. (These needles are known as "betweens.") For quilting with perle cotton or 12 weight cotton, use a good-quality crewel embroidery needle (I use a no. 9).

1. Thread the needle with about 18 in. (46 cm) of thread. Knot the end of the thread with a one-loop knot and take the needle down through the quilt top into the batting, a short distance from where you want to start quilting. Tug the thread slightly so that the knot pulls through the fabric into the batting, making the starting point invisible.

2. With your dominant hand above the quilt and the other beneath, insert the needle through all three layers at a time with the middle or index finger of your dominant hand (use a metal thimble to make this easier) until you can feel the tip of the needle resting on your finger at the back.

3. Without pushing the needle through, rock it back to the top of the quilt and use your underneath finger to push the tip up. Put your upper thumb down in front of the needle tip while pushing up from the back, as shown. This will make a small "hill" in the fabric.

4. Push the needle through the fabric. This makes one stitch. To take several stitches at once, push the needle along to the required stitch length, then dip the tip into the fabric and repeat the above technique. Gently pull the stitches to indent the stitch line evenly. You should always quilt toward yourself, as this reduces hand and shoulder strain, so turn the quilt in the required direction.

Tip You can protect your underneath finger using a stick-on plastic shield such as a Thimble-It. Or you could use a leather thimble, although this does make it more difficult to feel how far the needle has come through, and thus more difficult to keep your stitches neat and even. There is a free video of my hand-quilting technique available at the side of my blog (see page 157).

binding

Binding a quilt is the final stage of finishing it. The binding is the narrow strip of folded fabric that wraps around the outer edges of the quilt to hide the raw edges of the top, batting, and backing. For binding straight edges, as in most of the projects in this book, the strips can be cut either on the straight grain or on the bias, but if you are ever binding something with curves, such as a quilt with curved corners, or the Planting quilt (see pages 110–117), which has scalloped edges, the strips must be cut on the bias. There are various methods of binding a quilt, but the technique detailed here is how I like to bind mine.

1. From the width of the binding fabric, cut enough strips to equal the outside perimeter of your quilt, plus about 6 in. (15 cm) to allow for mitered corners and for the ends to be folded under. I cut my binding strips 3 in. (7.5 cm) wide and use a ½ in. (12 mm) seam when attaching them to the quilt.

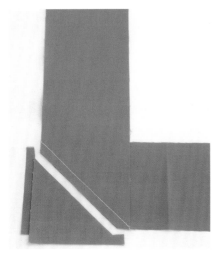 

2. To join the strips into a continuous length, first fold under one end of one strip at a 45-degree angle and finger-press a crease; unfold. The crease line will become the seam line, so mark this line lightly with a pencil. With right sides together and the two strips at 90 degrees, align the angled cut end with the next strip of binding fabric. Align the ¼ in. (6 mm) measurement on a quilter's ruler with this line and trim the corner. Sew the two strips together along the marked line. Press all seams to one side and trim off the "ears."

3. Press the entire strip in half along its length, with wrong sides together, as shown. Doubling the fabric like this makes the binding more durable.

4. Trim the backing and the batting so they are even with the edge of the quilt top. Beginning at one end of the binding strip, pin the binding to the right side of the quilt along one edge, starting about 4 in. (10 cm) in from a corner and aligning the raw edges. Attach a walking foot to your machine and machine-stitch the binding in place through all the layers of the quilt, using a ½-in. (12-mm) seam allowance, but leaving the first 1½ in. (4 cm) unstitched.

5. When you reach the first corner, you will need to miter the binding, so end the seam ½ in. (12 mm) from the corner and fasten off. Fold the remaining binding up at a 45-degree angle, and then fold it down so that the fold is level with the edge of the binding you have just sewn. Begin the next seam at the edge of the quilt and proceed as before.

6. Continue in the same way until you are approaching the point at which the binding started. Trim most of the excess, and turn back this end of the binding using a diagonal fold that runs in the same direction as the diagonal seams in the binding. Now tuck this turned-back end under the raw starting end, and stitch the rest of the seam.

7. Press the binding away from the quilt and turn it to the back of the quilt. Blind hemstitch it in place by hand along the seam line.

Adding a label
Once you have finished your quilt, you should add a label so that future generations know who made it—especially if the quilt is a gift. Pre-printed fabric labels are available to buy, or you could simply write on a nice piece of coordinating fabric with a laundry marker and slipstitch it to the back of the quilt.

templates

Most of the templates are full size and so do not need to be enlarged; they can simply be photocopied or traced. However, if it says to "enlarge to twice this size," you should enlarge it on a photocopier so that each dimension is twice as long as on the template shown. When instructions are given to add a seam allowance, you should add it to the fabric as you cut it out, not to the template.

i've got sunshine

(see pages 46–51)

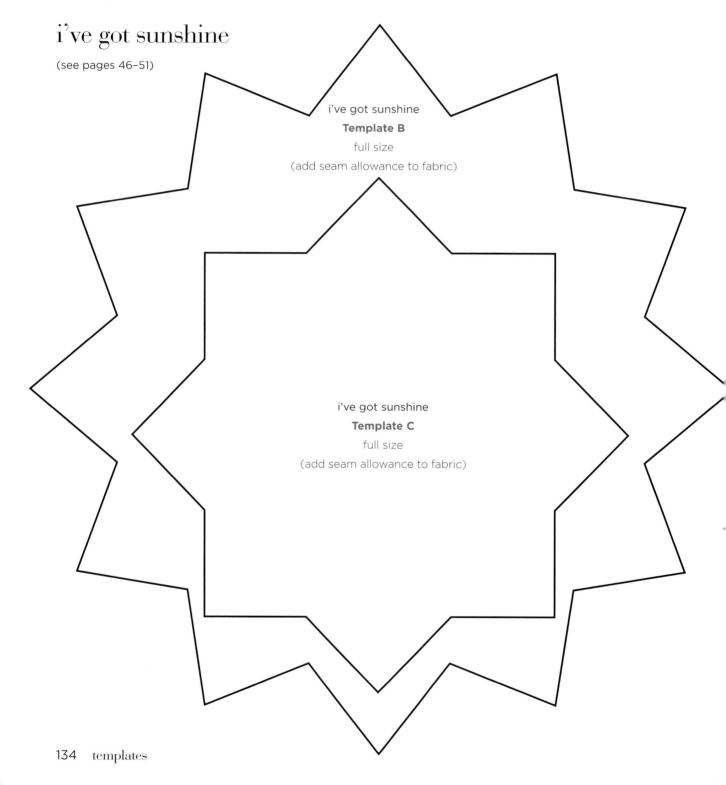

i've got sunshine
Template B
full size
(add seam allowance to fabric)

i've got sunshine
Template C
full size
(add seam allowance to fabric)

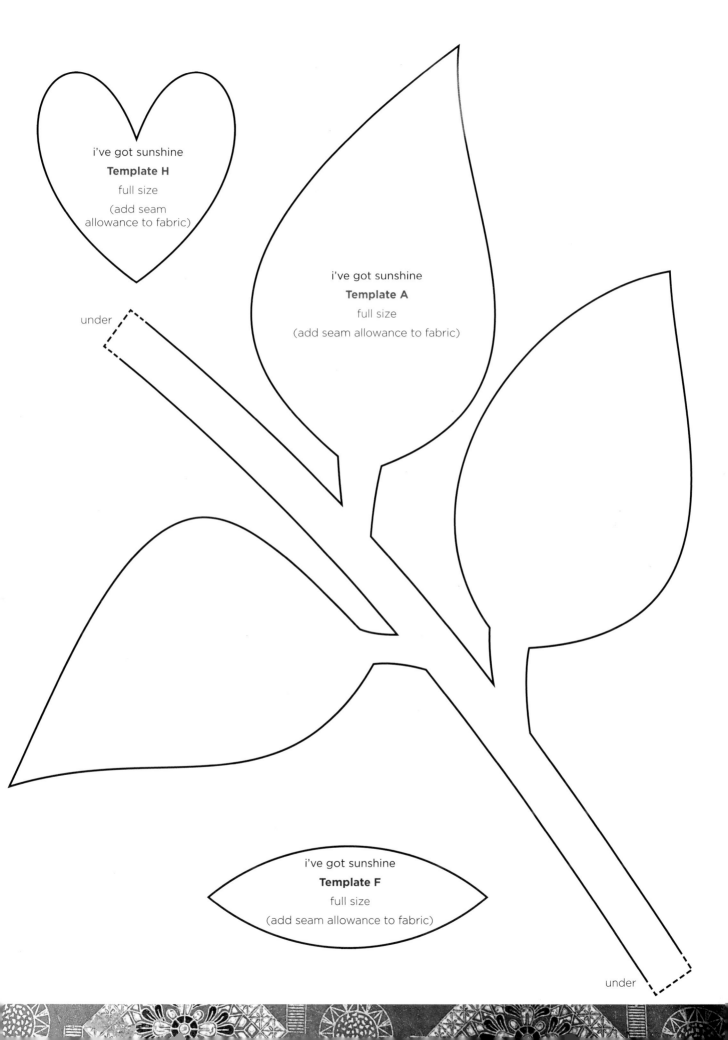

i've got sunshine

Template H

full size

(add seam
allowance to fabric)

under

i've got sunshine

Template A

full size

(add seam allowance to fabric)

i've got sunshine

Template F

full size

(add seam allowance to fabric)

under

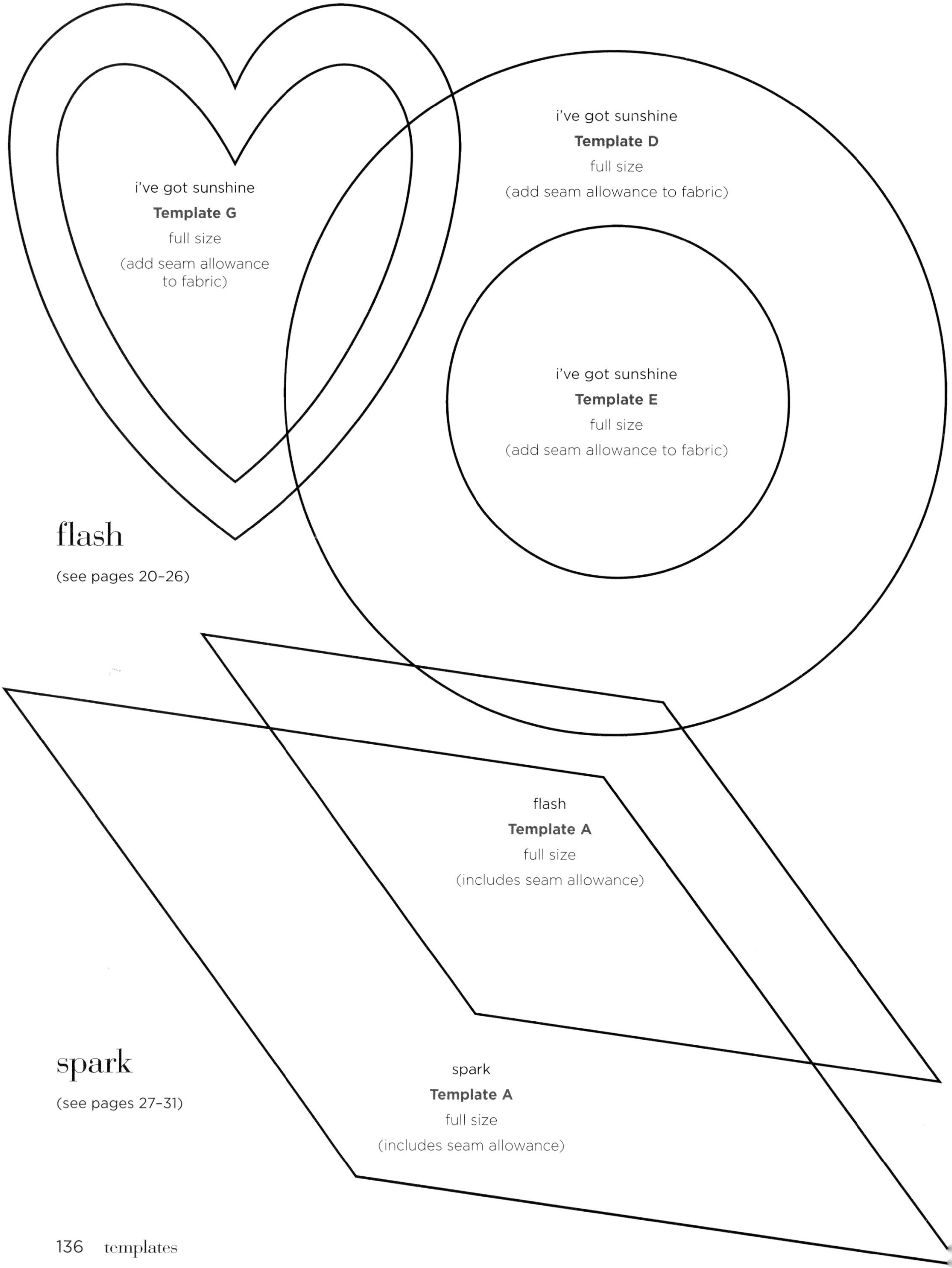

i've got sunshine
Template G
full size
(add seam allowance
to fabric)

i've got sunshine
Template D
full size
(add seam allowance to fabric)

i've got sunshine
Template E
full size
(add seam allowance to fabric)

flash

(see pages 20–26)

flash
Template A
full size
(includes seam allowance)

spark

(see pages 27–31)

spark
Template A
full size
(includes seam allowance)

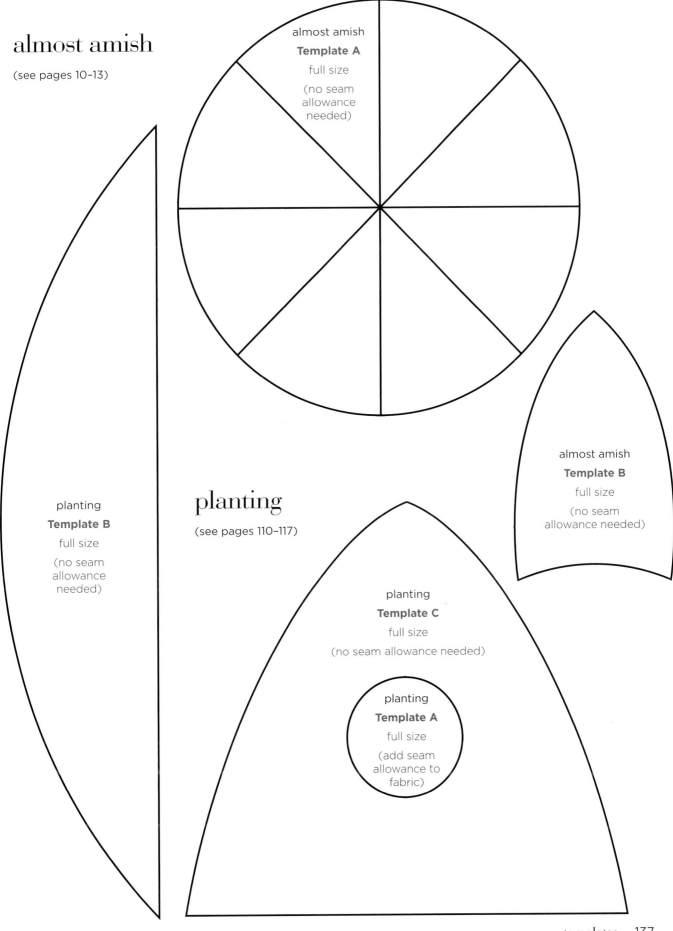

almost amish

(see pages 10–13)

almost amish
Template A
full size
(no seam allowance needed)

almost amish
Template B
full size
(no seam allowance needed)

planting
Template B
full size
(no seam allowance needed)

planting

(see pages 110–117)

planting
Template C
full size
(no seam allowance needed)

planting
Template A
full size
(add seam allowance to fabric)

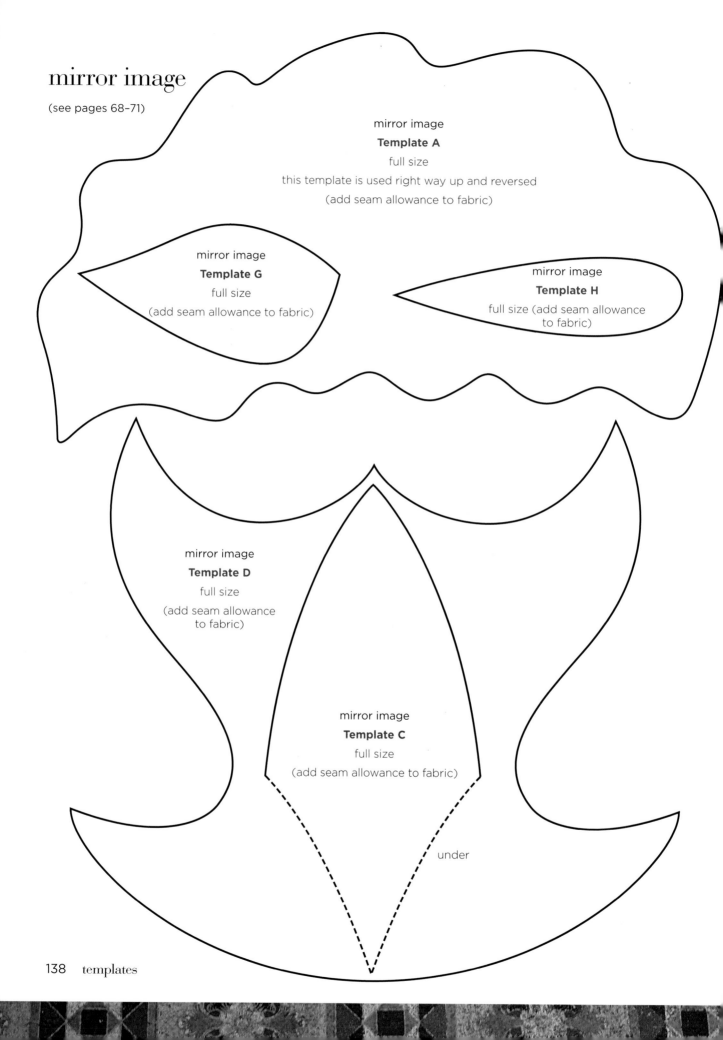

mirror image

(see pages 68–71)

mirror image
Template A
full size
this template is used right way up and reversed
(add seam allowance to fabric)

mirror image
Template G
full size
(add seam allowance to fabric)

mirror image
Template H
full size (add seam allowance
to fabric)

mirror image
Template D
full size
(add seam allowance
to fabric)

mirror image
Template C
full size
(add seam allowance to fabric)

under

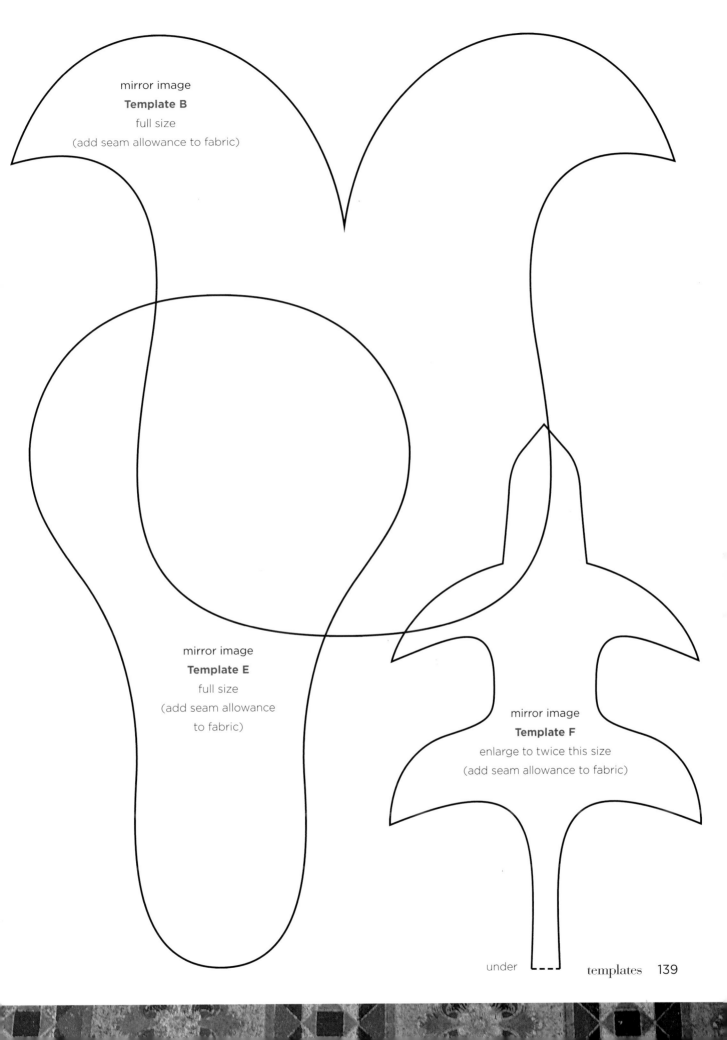

mirror image
Template B
full size
(add seam allowance to fabric)

mirror image
Template E
full size
(add seam allowance
to fabric)

mirror image
Template F
enlarge to twice this size
(add seam allowance to fabric)

under

pretty pinwheel

(see pages 118–123)

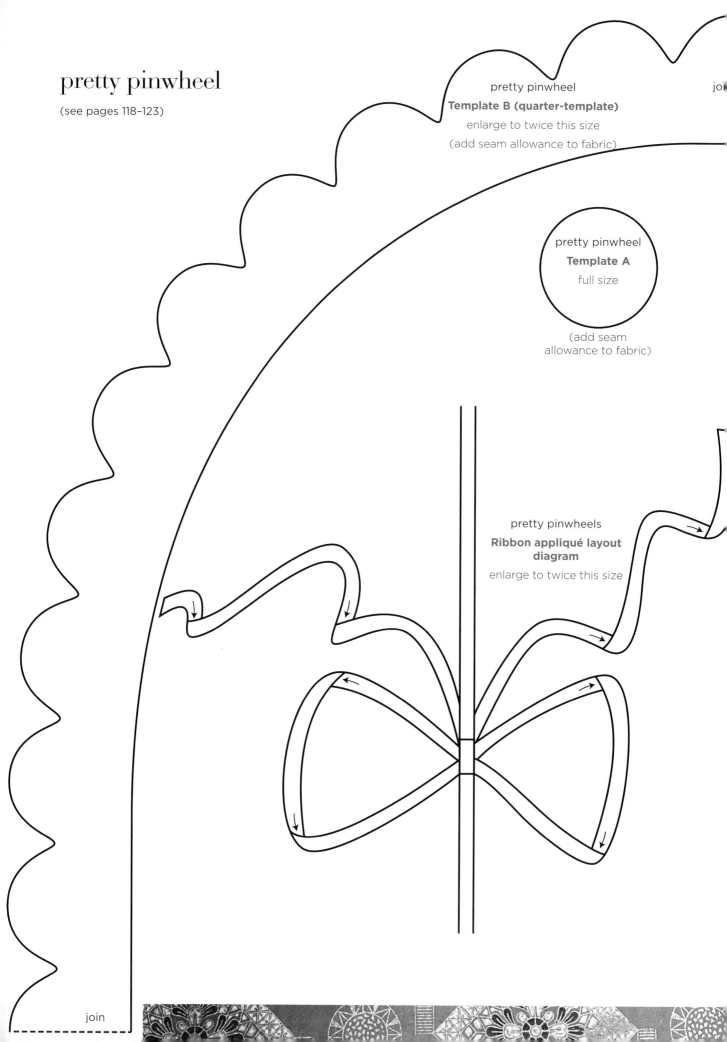

pretty pinwheel
Template B (quarter-template)
enlarge to twice this size
(add seam allowance to fabric)

jo

pretty pinwheel
Template A
full size

(add seam
allowance to fabric)

pretty pinwheels
**Ribbon appliqué layout
diagram**
enlarge to twice this size

join

smile, darn ya

(see pages 52-57)

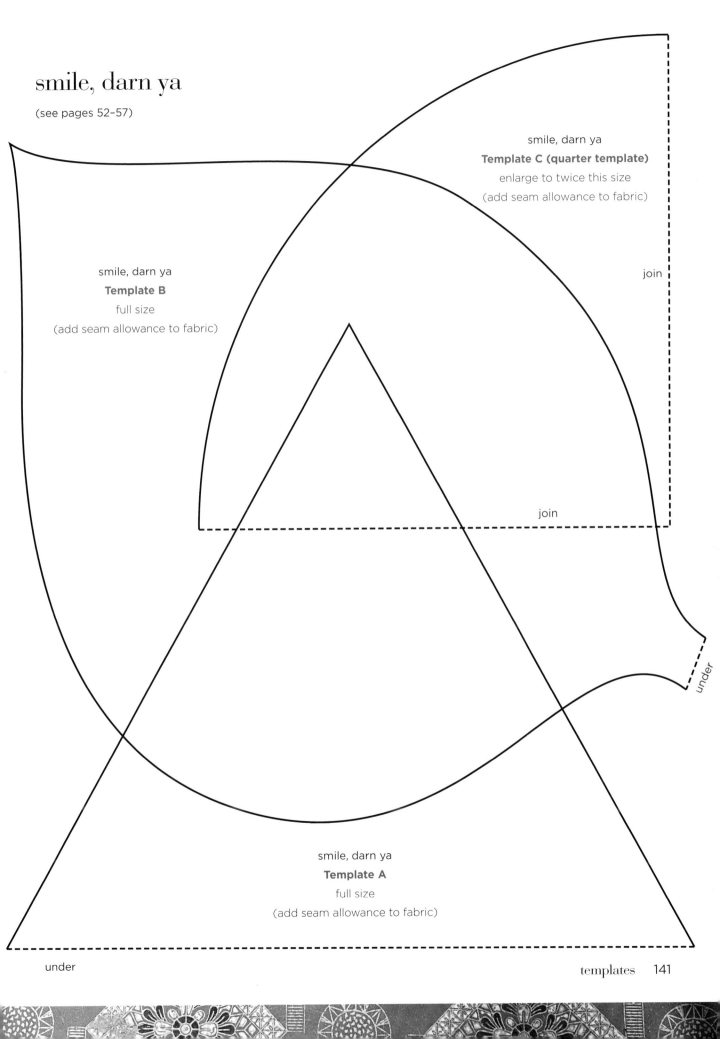

smile, darn ya
Template C (quarter template)
enlarge to twice this size
(add seam allowance to fabric)

join

smile, darn ya
Template B
full size
(add seam allowance to fabric)

join

under

smile, darn ya
Template A
full size
(add seam allowance to fabric)

under

sweet home

Template 2

full size

(add seam allowance
to fabric)

sweet home

Template 0

full size

(add seam allowance to fabric)

sweet home

Template 1

full size

(add seam
allowance
to fabric)

sweet home

(see pages 34–39)

sweet home

Template 5

full size

(add seam allowance to fabric)

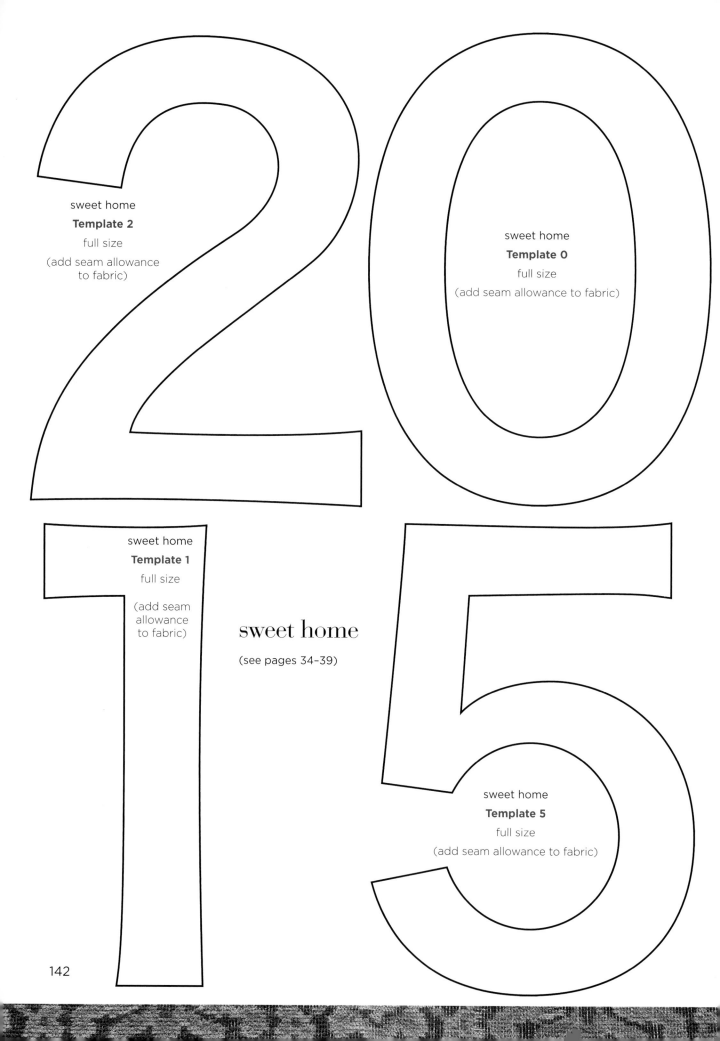

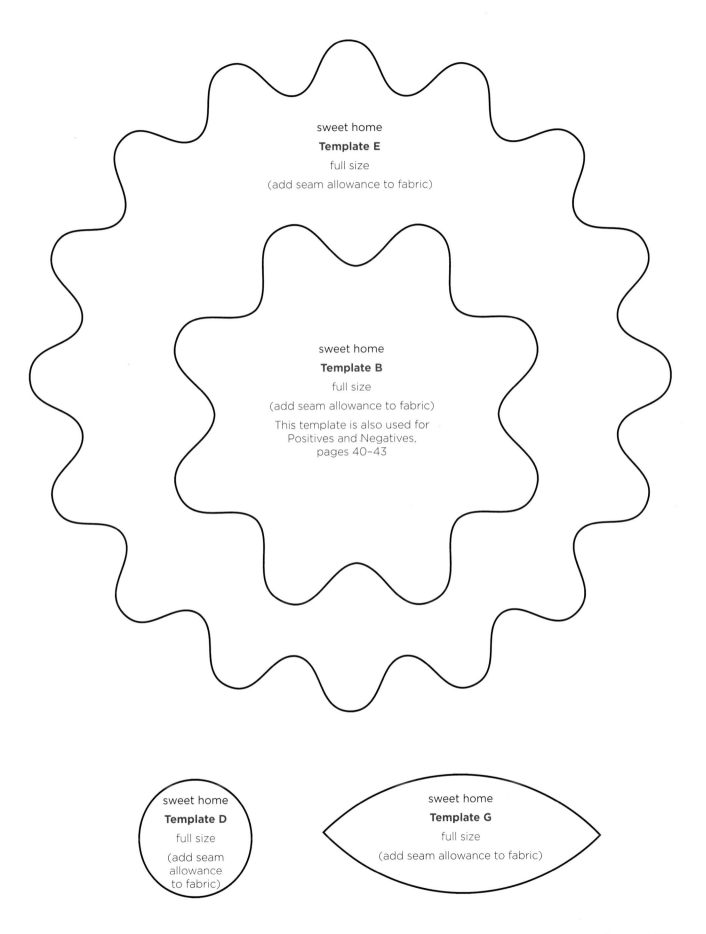

sweet home
Template E
full size
(add seam allowance to fabric)

sweet home
Template B
full size
(add seam allowance to fabric)
This template is also used for
Positives and Negatives,
pages 40–43

sweet home
Template D
full size
(add seam
allowance
to fabric)

sweet home
Template G
full size
(add seam allowance to fabric)

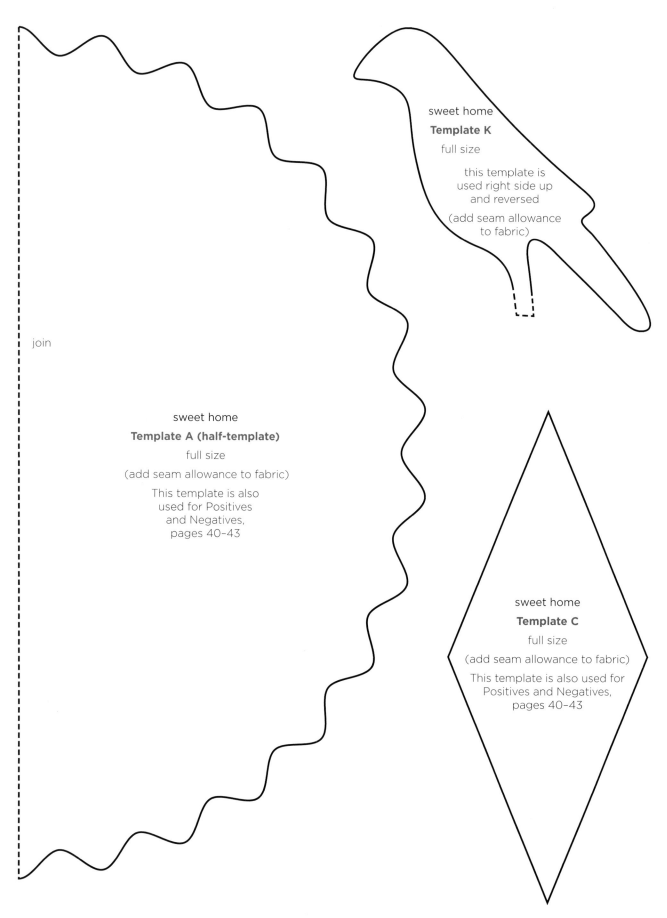

join

sweet home

Template K

full size

this template is
used right side up
and reversed

(add seam allowance
to fabric)

sweet home

Template A (half-template)

full size

(add seam allowance to fabric)

This template is also
used for Positives
and Negatives,
pages 40–43

sweet home

Template C

full size

(add seam allowance to fabric)

This template is also used for
Positives and Negatives,
pages 40–43

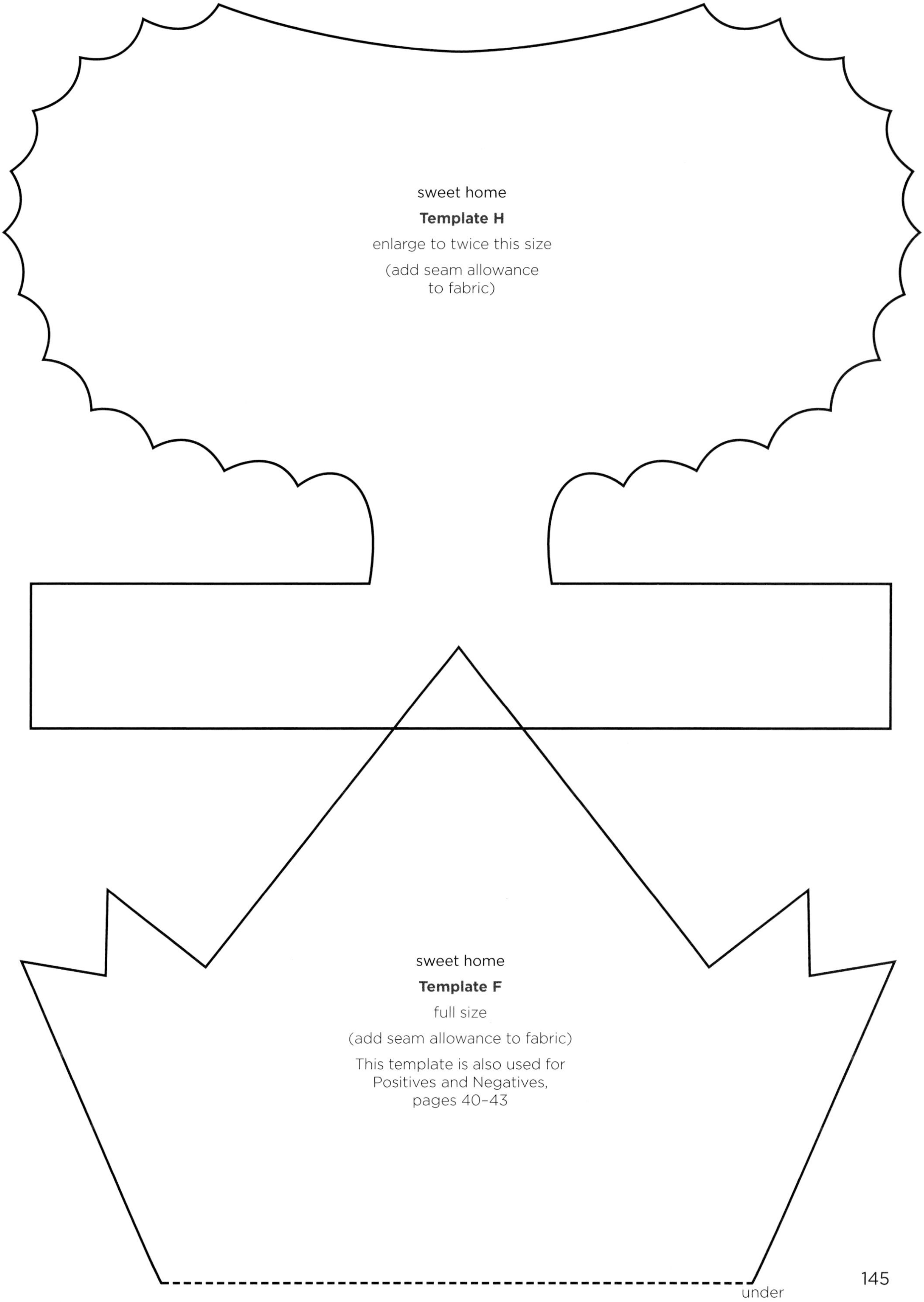

sweet home

Template H

enlarge to twice this size

(add seam allowance
to fabric)

sweet home

Template F

full size

(add seam allowance to fabric)

This template is also used for
Positives and Negatives,
pages 40–43

under

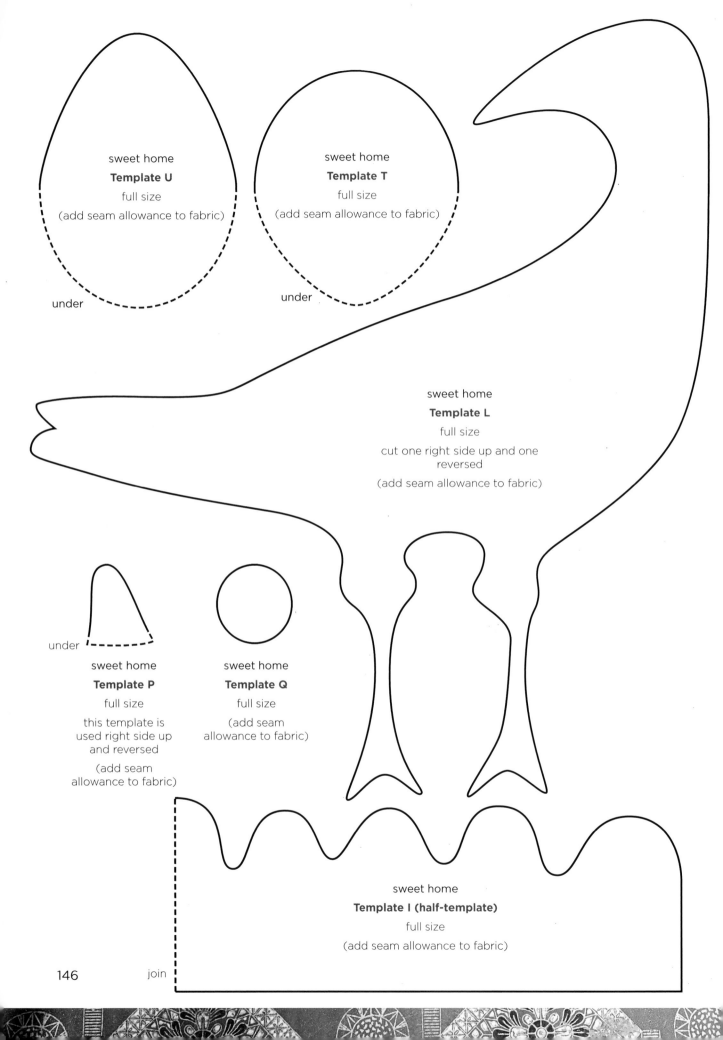

sweet home
Template U
full size
(add seam allowance to fabric)

under

sweet home
Template T
full size
(add seam allowance to fabric)

under

sweet home
Template L
full size
cut one right side up and one reversed
(add seam allowance to fabric)

under

sweet home
Template P
full size
this template is used right side up and reversed
(add seam allowance to fabric)

sweet home
Template Q
full size
(add seam allowance to fabric)

sweet home
Template I (half-template)
full size
(add seam allowance to fabric)

146

join

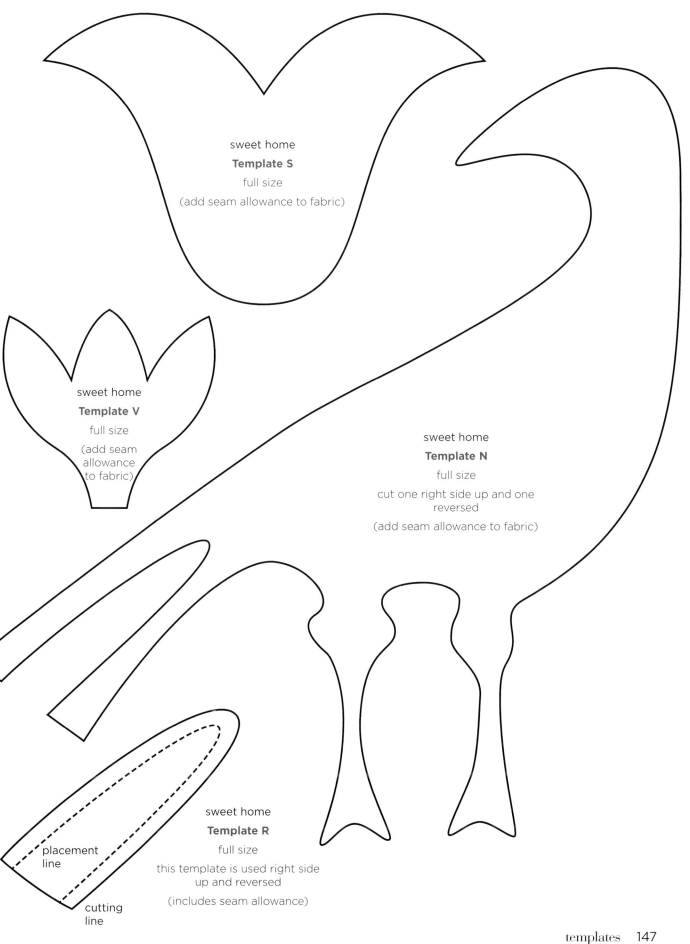

sweet home
Template S
full size
(add seam allowance to fabric)

sweet home
Template V
full size
(add seam allowance to fabric)

sweet home
Template N
full size
cut one right side up and one reversed
(add seam allowance to fabric)

placement line

cutting line

sweet home
Template R
full size
this template is used right side up and reversed
(includes seam allowance)

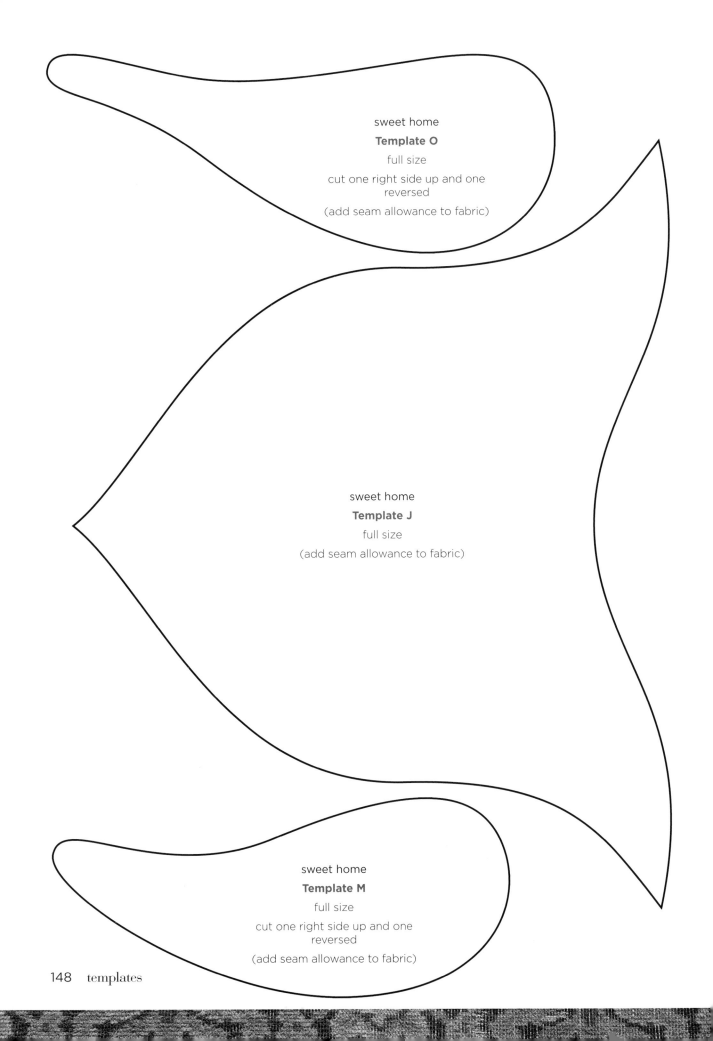

sweet home

Template O

full size

cut one right side up and one reversed

(add seam allowance to fabric)

sweet home

Template J

full size

(add seam allowance to fabric)

sweet home

Template M

full size

cut one right side up and one reversed

(add seam allowance to fabric)

2015

centenary

(see pages 60–67)

centenary

Date templates

full size

(add seam allowance to fabric)

centenary

Template A

full size

(add seam allowance to fabric)

under

centenary

Template B

full size

(add seam allowance to fabric)

under

centenary

Template C

full size

(add seam allowance to fabric)

centenary

Template E

full size

(add seam allowance to fabric)

centenary

Template F

full size

(add seam allowance to fabric)

under

centenary

Template D

full size

(add seam allowance to fabric)

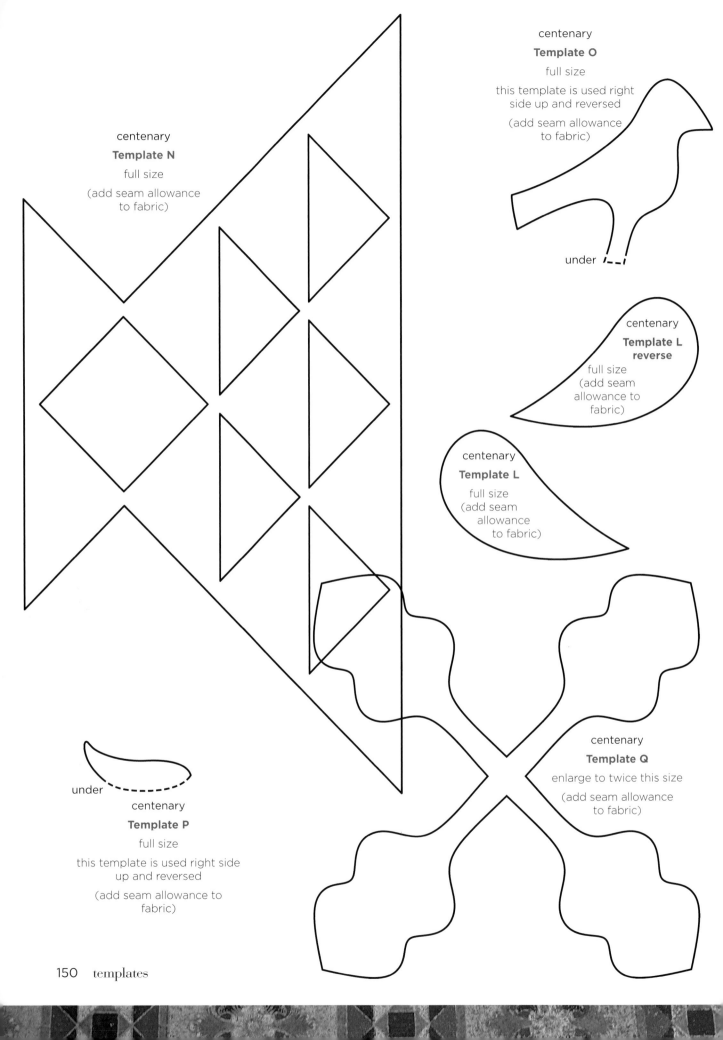

centenary

Template O

full size

this template is used right
side up and reversed

(add seam allowance
to fabric)

under

centenary

Template N

full size

(add seam allowance
to fabric)

centenary

**Template L
reverse**

full size
(add seam
allowance to
fabric)

centenary

Template L

full size
(add seam
allowance
to fabric)

centenary

Template Q

enlarge to twice this size

(add seam allowance
to fabric)

under

centenary

Template P

full size

this template is used right side
up and reversed

(add seam allowance to
fabric)

centenary

Template H reverse

full size

(add seam
allowance
to fabric)

centenary

Template H

full size

(add seam
allowance to
fabric)

centenary

Template S

enlarge to twice this size

(add seam allowance to fabric)

centenary

Template M

full size

(add seam
allowance to fabric)

centenary

Template M reverse

full size

(add seam
allowance to fabric)

centenary

Placement Diagram for Tulip Block

enlarge to twice this size

centenary
Template T
full size
(add seam allowance to fabric)

centenary
Template V
full size
(add seam allowance to fabric)

centenary
Template U
full size
(add seam allowance
to fabric)

centenary
Template G
full size
(add seam
allowance
to fabric)

centenary
Template G reverse
full size
(add seam
allowance
to fabric)

centenary
Template R
full size
(add seam allowance
to fabric)

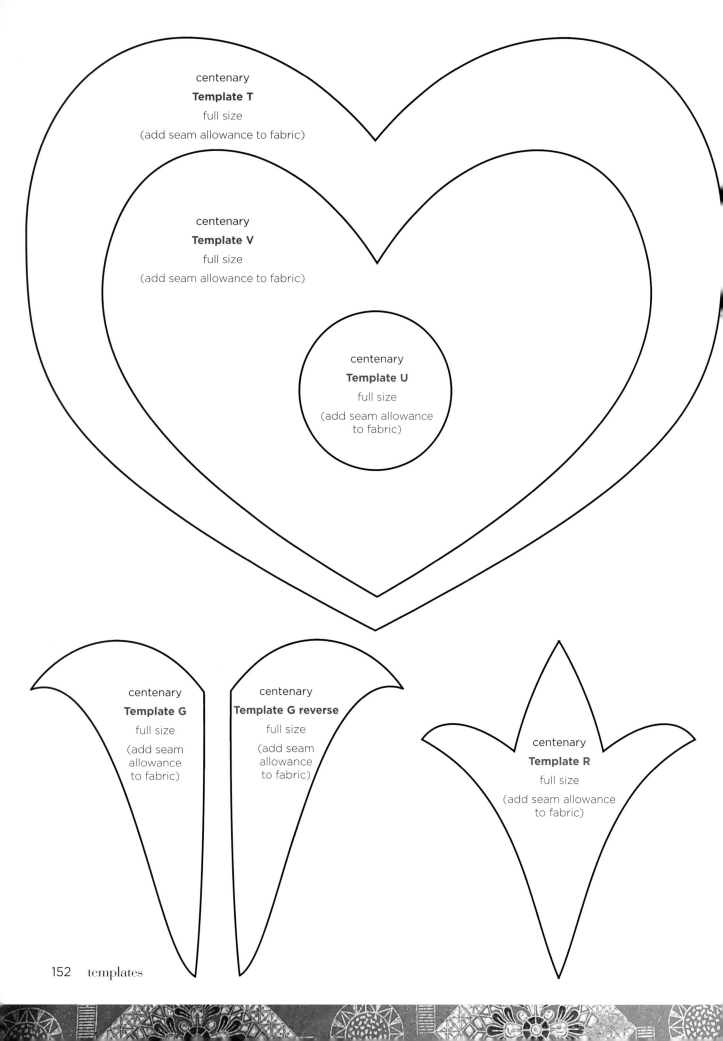

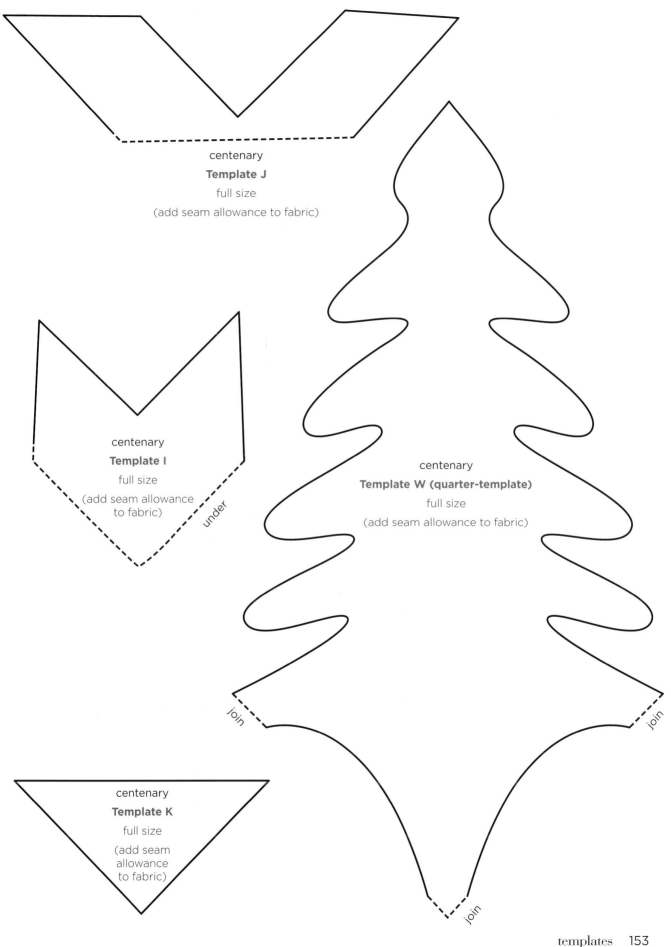

centenary
Template J
full size
(add seam allowance to fabric)

centenary
Template I
full size
(add seam allowance
to fabric)

under

centenary
Template W (quarter-template)
full size
(add seam allowance to fabric)

join

join

join

centenary
Template K
full size
(add seam
allowance
to fabric)

glossary

Appliqué
A technique in which small pieces of fabric are stitched to a background fabric.

Backing
The undermost layer of a quilt.

Basting (tacking)
A method of holding together several layers of fabric during quilting, so that they do not move around. Basting may be done using a long hand stitch, or with safety pins. The stitches or pins are removed once the quilting is complete.

Batting (wadding)
The middle layer of a quilt.

Bias
The diagonal of a woven fabric, at a 45-degree angle to the straight grain (the warp and weft). Fabric cut on the bias stretches, so care must be taken when handling and sewing bias-cut pieces. Compare with *grain*.

Binding
The narrow strips of fabric (usually made of a double thickness) that enclose the raw edges and batting of a quilt.

Block
The basic unit of a patchwork quilt top. Blocks are usually square, but may be rectangular, hexagonal, or other shapes. They may be plain (of one fabric only), appliquéd, or pieced.

Border
A strip of fabric (plain, appliquéd, or pieced) joined to the central panel of a quilt and used to frame it and also to add extra size.

Chain-piecing
A method of joining fabric pieces by machine in an assembly-line fashion, which speeds up the process and uses less thread. Pairs or sets of block pieces are fed into the machine, one after the other, without snipping the threads between them.

Cross-hatching
A quilting pattern of parallel equidistant lines that run in two directions to form a grid of squares or diamonds.

Design wall
A wall that displays pieces of a quilt top and allows you to view the progress of a quilt top from a distance. May be made from a piece of batting (wadding) or a flannel sheet pinned to the wall or a window.

Directional print
Printed fabric in which there is a distinct direction to the pattern, whether straight or at an angle; for example, stripes, human or animal figures, or some florals.

Ease
To make two pieces of fabric of different sizes fit together in a seam. One piece may have to be stretched or gathered slightly to bring it to the required length. To ease, first pin the pieces at intervals until they fit, then sew them.

Fat quarter and fat eighth
A fat quarter is a piece of fabric that is made by cutting a yard or a meter of fabric in halves vertically and then horizontally. Because the width of the fabric from selvage to selvage is 42–44 in. (107–112 cm), the piece thus cut is approximately 18 x 22 in. (50 x 56 cm). A fat eighth is a fat quarter cut in half to approximately 18 x 11 in. (50 x 28 cm).

Finger-pressing
A way of pressing a temporary crease in a piece of fabric, for example when finding the middle of two pieces so that they can be matched before being joined. Running a fingernail along a crease will make it lie flat.

Fussy cut
To cut out a pieced shape centered on a printed motif on the fabric, rather than cutting it out at random.

Grain
The direction of the fabric, along the warp (vertical threads) or the weft (horizontal threads). These are both straight grains, along which woven fabrics do not stretch. Compare with *bias*.

Half-square triangle
A triangle that is made from a square cut across one diagonal. Half-square triangles have the bias along the hypotenuse (or longest side). Compare with *quarter-square triangle*.

Mitered corner
A corner that is joined at a 45-degree angle.

Novelty print
A fabric printed with themed designs, such as toys, cartoon characters, or animals.

On point
An arrangement in which the quilt blocks are placed diamond fashion, with their corners at the 12, 3, 6, and 9 o'clock positions, rather than in a square fashion.

Outline-quilt
To make one or more outlines of a motif or block design, radiating outward.

Patchwork
A generic term for the process of sewing together many small pieces of fabric to make a quilt; also known as piecework.

Piece
An individual fabric shape that may be joined to other fabric shapes to make a quilt block, or used on its own (in which case it is known as a one-patch). Also known as a patch.

Piecing
The process of joining together pieces of fabric to make a quilt top, a quilt block, or a border.

Pin-baste
To pin through the layers of a quilt "sandwich," using safety pins, to hold them together during quilting. The pins are removed once the quilting is complete.

Quarter-square triangle
A triangle that is made from a square, cut across both diagonals. Quarter-square triangles have the bias along the two short sides. Compare with *half-square triangle*.

Quilt top
The uppermost, decorative layer of a quilt. It may be pieced, appliquéd, or a combination of both, with or without borders.

Quilter's ruler
Precision-cut, straight-edged plastic rulers in various sizes, used with rotary cutters and rotary-cutting (self-healing) mats. They make it easy to cut accurate shapes and to cut through several layers of fabric at once. They come in straight varieties and also those designed for cutting at various angles or for creating triangles.

Quilting
In general, the process of making a quilt; more specifically, the process of stitching patterns by hand or machine through the quilt layers to decorate the quilt, add strength, and anchor the batting (wadding) inside the quilt.

Quilting frame
A free-standing floor apparatus, made of wood or plastic tubing, in which a quilt is held while it is being quilted.

Quilting hoop
A hand-held circular wooden device in which a quilt is held while being quilted.

Raw edge
The cut edge of a fabric.

Reverse appliqué
An appliqué technique in which the motif is stitched to the underside of the background. The top fabric is then cut away inside the stitching line and the edges turned under to reveal the motif behind.

Rotary cutter
A cutting device similar in appearance to a pizza cutter, with a razor-sharp circular blade. Used in conjunction with a quilter's ruler and quilting mat, it allows several layers of fabric to be cut at once, easily and with great accuracy.

Rotary-cutting mat
A self-healing plastic mat on which a rotary cutter is used. It protects both the blade of the cutter and the work surface beneath the mat during cutting.

Sashing
Strips of fabric that separate blocks in a quilt, to frame them and/or make the quilt larger.

Seam allowance
The margin of fabric between the cut edge and seam line. For quilting and most appliqué, it is ¼ in. (6 mm).

Seam line
The guideline that is followed while sewing, or the stitching line joining layers of fabric.

Selvages
The woven finished edges along the length of the fabric.

Setting
The way in which blocks are arranged in a quilt top—for example, square or on point.

Setting square
A plain block or square used with pieced or appliquéd blocks in a quilt top.

Setting triangle
A triangle placed between blocks along the sides of a quilt set on point, to straighten up the edges.

Stash
A quilter's hoard of fabrics.

Template
Plastic, card, or paper shape used for tracing and cutting fabric pieces for piecing or appliqué or to transfer quilting designs to a quilt top.

Warp
The lengthwise threads in a woven fabric, which interlock with the weft threads; see also *weft*.

Weft
The widthwise threads in a woven fabric, which interlock with the warp threads; see also *warp*.

resources

I'm a big fan of shopping at my local quilt shop. Where possible, I would always encourage you to shop at your local patchwork shop rather than buy online. I'm aware that this isn't always feasible but a local quilt shop will help you select your fabric, give you recommendations and hints, and offer great classes to help you along the way. They can't survive to hold your classes unless you also shop with them, and so many are going out of business as a result of online shopping. I am often asked about my favorite Aussie quilt shops, so here they are. I currently teach or have taught at them all, so if you stop in, be sure to say hi from me! Viva la Quilt Shop!

Cottage Quiltworks in Mona Vale, NSW
Steph's Patchwork in Moruya, NSW
Precious Time in Toowoomba, QLD
Amitié Textiles in Melbourne, VIC
Cotton Factory in Ballarat, VIC

Fabric online

Obviously, listing every quilt shop is not possible, so here are a few online shops I like to visit (they ship worldwide).

New patchwork fabric online
Polka Dot Tea
www.etsy.com/au/shop/PolkaDot
TeaFabrics
Pink Castle Fabrics
www.pinkcastlefabrics.com
Fabricworm
www.fabricworm.com
Hawthorne Threads
www.hawthornethreads.com
Sunny Day Supply
www.sunnydayfabric.com
Miss Matatabi
www.etsy.com/au/shop/MissMatatabi

Vintage fabric and feedsacks online
The Crafty Squirrel
www.thecraftysquirrel.com.au
Sew Deerly Loved
www.etsy.com/shop/sewdeerlyloved
Vintage Sheet Variety
www.etsy.com/au/shop/VintageSheet
Variety
RickRack
www.rickrack.com

Worn and Washed
www.wornandwashedfabrics.com
Etsy and eBay are both treasure troves for vintage fabrics.

Solid fabrics online
Oakshott
www.oakshottfabrics.com
Rowan Shot Cottons
www.gloriouscolor.com
Simply Solids
www.simplysolids.co.uk

Liberty fabrics online
Lots of online shops have Liberty clubs and that is a fantastic way to build a Liberty stash in small pieces. These shops include Polka Dot Tea and Pink Castle Fabrics (see above).

Yardage online
Tessuti Fabrics
www.tessuti.com.au
Shaukat and Company
www.shaukat.co.uk

Notions (haberdashery)

The question I am asked most when I travel to teach is, what brand do I use? There are thousands of great products out there, but these are the brands I prefer at the moment.

For appliqué
• Tulip Milliners needles #11
• Aurifil Cotton Mako' Ne 50 weight thread
• Patchwork with Busy Fingers appliqué glue

For quilting
• Tulip Crewel Embroidery needles #10
• Presencia Finca Perle 8 cotton or Aurifil Mako' Ne 12 weight cotton
• Clover open-sided thimble
• Bonwick quilting hoop
• Matilda's Own 100% cotton batting (wadding)

Credits

Many of the patterned fabrics in Centenary and Ink Pink are thanks to my lovely friends Alexia, Sarah, Kim, Rashida, and Melody at Cotton and Steel. Thanks to Oakshott Fabrics for the solids in A Stitch in Time and Almost Amish.

Thank you to Alison Glass and Windham Fabrics for sending lovely parcels of fabrics that have been worked into my designs. All threads used in the hand-quilting and appliqué are thanks to lovely Alex at Aurifil.

Picture credits

The photographs on the following pages are reproduced with permission from the American Folk Art Museum and can be found, along with many others, in the wonderful book *Quilts: Masterworks from the American Folk Art Museum* by Elizabeth V. Warren: page 8; page 18 by Terry McGinnis; page 32 by Matt Hoebermann; page 44 by Matt Hoebermann; page 58; page 72 by Gavin Ashworth; page 84 by Gavin Ashworth; page 96 by Schecter Lee; page 108 by Gavin Ashworth.

Perspex ruler sets

Perspex ruler sets are available from me for the following quilts in this book:

Flash
Spark
Sweet Home
Positives and Negatives
I've Got Sunshine
Mosaic
Ebb and Flow
Ink Pink
Keep It Down
Planting
Pretty Pinwheel

The ruler sets are also available for quilts in my previous books. In addition, I sell the tools mentioned for appliqué and quilting, including Australian-made quilting hoops, my fabric ranges for Lecien, Spotlight, and Windham Fabrics, my thread collections for Aurifil, scrap bags, and all my books.

Visit me at www.sarahfielke.com—and, yes, I ship worldwide.

Blogs & websites about quilts

Inspirational
Bemused
www.bemused.typepad.com
Mrs Schmenkman Quilts
www.mrsschmenkmanquilts.word
press.com
Pam Kitty Morning
www.pamkittymorning.blogspot.com
Piece and Press
www.pieceandpress.blogspot.com
Quiltville
www.quiltville.blogspot.com

About antique quilts
Barbara Brackman
www.barbarabrackman.blogspot.com
International Quilt Study Center & Museum
www.quiltstudy.org
The National Quilt Museum
www.quiltmuseum.org

About modern quilting
The Modern Quilt Guild
www.themodernquiltguild.com
Jackie Gering
www.tallgrassprairiestudio.blogspot.com

Find me online

I love answering questions and hearing from those of you who have made my quilts or enjoyed my books. Come and say hi!
Website: www.sarahfielke.com
Blog: www.thelastpiece.net
Email: sarah@sarahfielke.com
Twitter: @sarahfielke
Facebook: /sarah.fielke
Pinterest: sarahfielke
Instagram: sfielke
See my blog at www.thelastpiece.net for free video tutorials on Perfect Circle Appliqué, Making Bias Strips, and Hand Quilting. You can take an online class with me in appliqué and using specialty rulers at www.craftsy.com.

Teaching

I teach regular classes in Sydney, and I often teach interstate and overseas. I teach online classes at Craftsy.com. You can find all the details of my latest classes on my blog, or email me to ask for a class list if you would like me to visit your local shop or group.

index

about the location

The idea for this book has been so strong in my mind for such a long time, and one of the things I really wanted to show was the new, bright designs and modern fabrics in an old house, somewhere in keeping with the period of the original quilts. Old meets new, the past and the present. Glowing new colors against faded, soft colors of age. Finding a venue was not easy, but my wonderful photographer Sue Stubbs discovered Craigmoor at Hill End in New South Wales.

Craigmoor was built in 1875 during the gold rush in Australia. It is believed the house was built in the style of a hunting lodge in Scotland where James Wiseman Marshall, the owner, grew up. The house was grand for its day, and James and his wife Sarah lived there for over 20 years with their 12 children.

What Sue and I didn't realize until we got to the house and started looking around, was that the Marshall girls, Maude, Hannah, Janet, Caroline, and Mary Agnes, and their mother Sarah, were quilters, and indeed stitchers of all kinds. The house is full to bursting with embroidery, tapestries, old sewing notions, and machines. And, on nearly all the beds, quilts.

The quilts at Craigmoor are mostly thought to have been made from around the mid-1870s through to the 1940s. Many of the quilts contain pieces of cloth from family members' clothing. Each quilt has been placed on the bed in the bedroom of the person for whom it was made. With the amazing foresight of James and Sarah's grandson, when the last of the family left the house in 1975, objects were left just as they were when the house was occupied by the young Marshall family.

After spending three days shooting my quilts in this special surrounding, I felt I couldn't have found a more amazing piece of quilter's past to showcase my quilts of the present.

acknowledgments

Thanks must go to:

Erica Spinks, my lovely friend and trusted editor—and emergency binder!—who always has a word of wisdom and time for a coffee.

Sue Stubbs, photographer extraordinaire and sometime quilt wrangler, who always makes my quilts look so beautiful and my days at photography shoots so fun and creative.

Jayne Rennie of Quilting Finesse, for doing such a beautiful job on the machine quilting and being so willing and available at the 11th hour.

Sandy Caller, stunt binder to the stars.

Kim Bradley for quilting A Stitch in Time.

Jeanette Bruce for quilting Ink Pink.

Matt and his team at NSW National Parks and Wildlife Service in Hill End for access to the wonderful sites in the town;

Sandra Thompson at NSW National Parks and Wildlife Service for her help at Craigmoor and the wonderful information about the house and the family.

Miriam Catley, Sally Powell, Penny Craig, and Cindy Richards at CICO Books, plus Gillian Haslam and Alison Wormleighton, for their help, support, design, editing, and all around wonderfulness.

Charlie and Oscar, for always reminding me to come out of the fabric fog and be with my family.

The LMGTFY group for the laughs. You know who you are.

All the quilty peeps far and near, in class, online, and those I've never met. Your enthusiasm and words of encouragement are what keeps me going! Huzzah for the quilters!